University of Manitoba Press
Winnipeg, Manitoba R3T 2N2 Canada
www.umanitoba.ca/uofmpress
Printed in Canada on acid-free paper by Friesens.

Cover Design: Doowah Design
Text Design: Sharon Caseburg
Cover Photo: Greg Klassen

National Library of Canada Cataloguing in Publication Data

Riegel, Christian Erich, 1968-
  Writing grief : Margaret Laurence and the work of mourning / Christian Riegel.

  Includes bibliographical references and index.
  ISBN 0-88755-673-6

  1. Laurence, Margaret, 1926-1987--Criticism and interpretation. 2. Grief in literature. I. Title.
PS8523.A86Z825 2003   C813'.54   C2003-911068-0

The University of Manitoba Press gratefully acknowledges the financial support for its publication program provided by the Government of Canada through the Book Publishing Industry Development Program (BPIDP); the Canada Council for the Arts; the Manitoba Arts Council; and the Manitoba Department of Culture, Heritage and Tourism.

This book has been published with the help of a grant from the Canadian Federation for the Humanities and Social Sciences, through the Aid to Scholarly Publications Programme, using funds provided by the Social Sciences and Humanities Research Council of Canada.

WRITING GRIEF

WRITING GRIEF

*Margaret Laurence
and the Work of Mourning*

Christian Riegel

UNIVERSITY OF MANITOBA PRESS

MAR 3 (

For Katherine

CONTENTS

ACKNOWLEDGEMENTS

In the writing of this book I was fortunate to have the support of a number of people. Doug Barbour provided thoughtful and stimulating critique at key moments. I am indebted to Nora Foster Stovel for her insightful reading of my work during an earlier phase of writing. I am fortunate to have had the benefit of James King's insight into Laurence's biography and writing, and of his particularly supportive response to my work.

I am thankful to my friends and colleagues who, by their presence in my life at various times over the years, made the work interesting and sustainable: Len Falkenstein, Erika Rothwell, Karen Overbye, Jeanette Lynes, and Birk Sproxton. Nat Hardy provided the kind of support at a critical time in the writing that goes beyond friendship and that mere thanks do not do justice to. Thanks also to Jerilyn Ninowski, my research assistant, for invaluable help with final manuscript preparation. I would like to thank Tracy Ware and David Baron for fostering my passion for literary studies. I am also grateful for the encouragement of my family, Dieter, Jutta, and Henriette Riegel.

Jonathan Hart has offered his profound intellectual and personal generosity: he inspires and mentors through his dedication to scholarship, and all the while he does so with great humanity. During the times when there seemed to be no end in sight, this support is what carried the work.

I am grateful to David Carr for the interest he showed in developing this book and ultimately bringing it to press; and also to Patricia Sanders, my editor, for her astute handling of textual matters.

Finally, I thank Katherine Robinson for her ability to make plain the underlying structures in my writing, a thankless task if there ever was one, and for so thoroughly enriching my life.

Chapter 4 was published in a different form under the same title in *Challenging Territory: The Writing of Margaret Laurence*, ed. Christian Riegel (Edmonton: University of Alberta Press, 1997), 67-80.

WRITING GRIEF

INTRODUCTION

MOURNING, WORK, AND LIMINALITY
IN THE MANAWAKA FICTION

> One should not develop a taste for mourning, and yet
> mourn we *must*.
>
> We *must*, but we must not like it—mourning, that is,
> mourning *itself*, if such a thing exists: not to like or love
> through one's own tear but only through the other, and
> every tear is from the other, the friend, the living, as long
> as we ourselves are living, reminding us, in holding like,
> to hold on to it.
>
> Jacques Derrida, *The Work of Mourning*

The themes of death, dying, and the reaction to such losses—
generally encompassed by the term *mourning*[1]—are significant
in the history of literary expression. Early examples of such
writing are found in Greek tragedy, as in the works of

Aeschylus, Euripides, and Sophocles. Since then, writers in each major period have focussed on death and mourning, including representative writers such as Dante,[2] Shakespeare, Gray, Wordsworth, Tennyson, and Tolstoy, to cite just a few. The twentieth century is notable for the intense and self-conscious interest writers have shown in this subject, ranging from the poetic elegies of Hardy, Eliot, Stevens, Auden, and Plath to the prose writings of Lawrence, Joyce, Woolf, and Mann.

Although Margaret Laurence has long been recognized as a central figure in Canadian writing generally, and while her Manawaka fiction is Canadian in its geographical, historical, and socio-cultural specificity,[3] it can also be placed within the larger tradition of writing that explores and figures death and mourning. Laurence's oeuvre prefigures important work by female Canadian novelists such as Alice Munro, Mavis Gallant, Joy Kogawa, and Jane Urquhart[4] in this area, and novels by other writers such as Margaret Drabble, Ann Beattie, and Jessica Anderson, for example.

Not only are death and mourning pervasive in Laurence's writing, but her personal life was deeply informed by her first-hand experience of death. Her mother died of a kidney infection when Laurence was four and her father died of pneumonia when she was nine. James King notes, in his biography *The Life of Margaret Laurence*, that "More than anything else, Neepawa was primarily for Peggy a place of death."[5] He borrows the term "blood child" from Sylvia Fraser's Afterword to the New Canadian Library edition of *The Fire-Dwellers* to designate Laurence's childhood because "that shocking severance of the blood tie creates a psychic wound that time never heals." King notes that, throughout her life, "Her jovial exterior was genuine, but it concealed the tormented inner little girl who had suffered the trauma of the loss of both birth parents."[6]

In her memoir *Dance on the Earth*, published posthumously, Laurence repeatedly notes her mother's death as a distinct absence in the first chapter, titled "Forewords." Her second chapter is titled with her mother's first name, Verna, and recounts her first memory, which is based on visiting her mother as she lies ill on what was to become her deathbed. She remarks on the foundational qualities of that first memory: "This memory is my first conscious one, my own memory rather than the imagined memories of infanthood and early childhood that were based on what is told to me later on."[7] The emotion evident in Laurence's recollection in the memoir, written nearly fifty years after the event, asserts the significance of her early experience of parental loss and reinforces the significance of Laurence's young experiences of the devastation of death:

> My mother, lying in the grey-painted double bed, smiles at me. Her face is white and her dark hair is spread out across the white pillowcase. She touches my face, my hair.
>
> It is unlikely she knew she was dying. Or perhaps she did know, or suspected, and it broke her heart to leave us, my father and me, and her sisters and beloved mother. I hope she didn't know. But I have no memory of anything more complicated than the look of love for me. I never saw her again.[8]

Laurence's description focusses on the elements that are clearly lost to her forever: the benevolent and loving mother whose last gesture is to express love for her young daughter and the touch of her mother's hand on her head and hair. Both elements link closely to the primary impulses of the mourner who is engaged in attempts to recreate or bring back—even if only fleetingly—that which has been lost. For Laurence, this work of mourning involved writing fictional texts that explored autobiographical material.

Laurence's exploration of death and mourning in all five texts in the Manawaka cycle underscores the pain of loss and the struggle to come to grips with it.[9] Autobiographical in impulse, although clearly fictional, these books serve in part as an exploration of Laurence's deep-rooted fascination with death,[10] but they also function as significant commentary on the relation of the individual in the western world to the discourses of death and mourning in the mid- to late twentieth century.

Laurence had a keen interest in the effects of death on the daily lives of the survivors. As Morag Gunn affirms in *The Diviners*, death and life are closely, yet uneasily, linked, and, while death is physically final, memories of the deceased will continue to affect the living in significant ways: "*I remember their deaths, but not their lives. Yet they're inside me, flowing unknown in my blood and moving unrecognized in my skull*" (27). Psychologist Peter Marris notes, in *Loss and Change*, that individuals "whose lives were intimately involved with the dead are faced by a radical disruption in the pattern of their relationships.... Bereavement presents unambiguously one aspect of social changes—the irretrievable loss of the familiar."[11]

In focussing specifically on the significance of the emotional responses to death and serious loss, generally termed mourning, I theorize the psychic responses to death as "work," and I do so in two central ways: work that needs doing, as in the psychological, social, and cultural processes of mourning themselves; and work that results from mourning, as in the creatively articulated texts that result from grief. I focus on the ways that Laurence's characters perform their work of mourning, and on how the mourning-work is initiated. Each of Laurence's protagonists finds herself in a state of liminality—an in-between state that demarcates a change in human development—and can only move through it by actively mourning.

Laurence demonstrates in all five books in the Manawaka series that the struggles of her protagonists to articulate their work of mourning, the move to conscious mourning, is a difficult one. In the first three novels—*The Stone Angel* (1964), *A Jest of God* (1966), and *The Fire-Dwellers* (1969)—the heroines labour to bring their emotions of loss to the surface so that they can be voiced, thus allowing the work of mourning to be performed. In the final books, *A Bird in the House* (1970) and *The Diviners* (1974), Laurence focusses on the self-reflexive work of mourning that her protagonists perform as they articulate it textually. In the last two books, the work of mourning is depicted as being both an aesthetic product and the mourning process itself that the characters undergo.

All five protagonists suffer under the weight of grief that shadows their lives, and has for many years in all cases. They must each, in their own ways, find the mechanism that will allow the work of mourning to occur. In a letter to the widow of his friend Max Loreau—the Belgian philosopher and writer—theorist Jacques Derrida writes of the immensity of the weight of loss he is feeling:

> This being at a loss says something, of course, about mourning and about its truth, the impossible mourning that nonetheless remains at work, endlessly hollowing out the depths of our memories, beneath their great beaches and beneath each grain of sand, beneath the phenomenal or public scope of our destiny and behind the fleeting, inapparent moments, those without archive and without words.[12]

Ever-present, ever-shadowed by the inescapability of loss, mourning continues but remains beyond conscious articulation in Derrida's conception. For Laurence's protagonists, the struggle is to address the loss and thus attempt redress, and to actively and forcefully engage the depths of grief in the work, the labour of mourning.

Mourning is complex, emotionally necessary, and has the aim of providing for the mourner much-needed consolation in the face of pain. Furthermore, the mourning situation is inherently socio-cultural and psychic in nature. According to sociologist David Mellor, it is a condition whereby an individual, in response to a death or serious loss, suffers the "shattering of a sense of ontological security."[13] A mourning individual will call into question "the meaningfulness and reality of the social frameworks in which they participate."[14] In her book *Grief as a Family Process*, psychologist Ester R. Shapiro argues that death in our culture "abandons family survivors of a loved one's death to a crisis of loss and a crisis of personal meaning . . . [and it] forces us to dissolve and recreate the deepest human bonds that form us."[15] Mourning is also a condition whereby the emotional investment in the deceased requires psychic response. Psychologist John Bowlby writes that

> [a]ll who have discussed *the nature of the processes engaged in healthy mourning* are agreed that amongst other things they effect, in some degree at least, a withdrawal of emotional investment in the lost person and that they may prepare for making a relationship with a new one [italics in original].[16]

Sigmund Freud, in his essay "Mourning and Melancholia," applied the term *decathexis* to describe mourning as the process of the release of the tie between an individual and the objects, especially other people, into which the mourner has invested emotional significance. Freud limited the time allowed for the successful completion of *decathexis* to approximately two years, considering mourning that went on for longer pathological and terming it "melancholia."[17] John Bowlby revises Freud's notion of a limited time for healthy mourning,[18] and agrees with literary critic Neal Tolchin that grief "surfaces when the environment or a psychic crisis triggers long-harbored ambivalent feelings toward the dead. . . . Until the mourner works through the conflicts he or she feels toward the deceased, a full cathartic grief reaction cannot occur."[19]

Freud's elucidation of mourning has further significance for the understanding of the Manawaka fiction, for Freud explored the resonances of the German word for mourning, *Trauerarbeit*, which is more fully encompassing than the English translation. In German the word is literally "mourning-work" and can mean "work of mourning," as in a text of mourning, or "the work that is required to mourn." Freud elaborated the second meaning most fully by using metaphors of work (as in labour) to define mourning, considering it "in terms of the economics of the mind."[20] Grief work is difficult and time-consuming.[21] Psychologist Robert Kastenbaum points out, echoing Freud, that "the work of grief. . . . is carried out through a long series of confrontations with the reality of the loss."[22]

Later thinkers extend Freud's conception of the possibility of the work of mourning, theorizing about the role of language in terms of the labour required. For grieving to be effective, the emotions of loss must be translated into words and must be articulated. The work of mourning, notes literary theorist and critic Robert Stamelman, "penetrates the being of language, filling it with a sorrow so abundant and . . . so fecund that the worded grief displaces the loved object, its source."[23] Derrida, in "By Force of Mourning," an essay written after the death of Louis Marin, the French semiotician, philosopher, and art historian, remarks on the intertwined nature of the work required in mourning and the work of articulation that results:

> Work: that which makes for a work, for an *oeuvre*, indeed
> that which works—and works to open: *opus* and *opening*,

oeuvre, and *ouverture*: the work or labor of the *oeuvre* insofar as it engenders, produces, and brings to light, but also labor or travail as suffering, as the engendering of force, as the pain of one who gives. Of the one who gives birth, who brings to the light of day and gives something to be seen, who enables or empowers, who gives the force to know and to be able to see—and all these are powers of the image, the pain of what is given and of the one who takes pains to help us see, read, and think.[24]

Laurence's mourners struggle to open themselves to grief, and must learn to do so before they are able to confront the weight of loss they experience in daily life. Derrida's sense of the labour of mourning as a process that brings to light emotions of loss is usefully applied to Laurence's protagonists as they each move to positive expressions of grief they previously were unable to externalize. Further, the idea of a labour of suffering in the action of mourning is significant for the main characters in the Manawaka fiction, as the labour of grief is achieved and carried out only with great difficulty and pain.

Laurence's characters must ultimately allow themselves to mourn, whether by breaking free of socially defined strictures, or of more personally, and thus privately, defined restrictions on active grief. In the same essay on Louis Marin, Derrida asks the question, "but what does one do when one works?" stating in his answer that part of the work involves giving oneself permission to perform the work of mourning, just as Laurence's protagonists must do in the Manawaka novels:

When one works *on* work, on the "work of mourning", when one works at the work of mourning, one is already, yes, already, *doing* such work, enduring this work of mourning from the very start, letting it work within oneself, and thus authorizing oneself to do it, according it to oneself, according it within oneself, and giving oneself this liberty of finitude, the most worthy and freest possible.[25]

Each of the five Manawaka texts is concerned with this notion of working towards articulating grief, or moving to *ouverture* and according the self the right to mourn, but the final two books also explore that articulation as aesthetic product—as a fictional work of mourning. The activities of the protagonists, Vanessa and Morag, are well defined by the words of Stamelman: "Writing is an act of survivorship; it is what the survivor does in order to keep on going, to understand what has happened in his or her life, and to give form, shape, and sound to the pain of losing."[26] Literary critic John J. Clayton argues, in *Gestures of Healing*, that "One way to see any expressive art is as an attempt to end discords in its creator—to express that experience and so gain control of it. Seen in this way, art isn't just a record of coping, it is an act of coping, *a gesture of healing*."[27]

In her essay "Time and the Narrative Voice," Laurence discusses the difficulty she faces in accurately conveying a sense of the time that supercedes what is easily written in the text: "In any work of fiction, the span of time present in the story is not only as long as the time-span of every character's life and memory; it also represents everything acquired and passed on in a kind of memory-heritage from one generation to another." She asks: "How can one even begin to convey this sense of time? What parts of the time-span should be conveyed?" Her answer is interesting in the context of the discussion of the work of mourning, for she attributes a period of uncertain contemplation before she begins writing fiction that revolves around these questions. What she terms "brooding" is akin to the movement to *ouverture* so evident in her characters' experiences. There is a parallel between how issues of time are eventually dealt with and how mourning is figured in the texts:

> before beginning any piece of writing, I tend to brood
> for quite a long time (clockwise) on these things. Not
> that brooding does very much good, usually, or perhaps

it bears fruit at some unrecognized subconscious level, because when the writing begins, a process of selection takes place in a way not consciously chosen.[28]

Interestingly, in these comments one sees an emphasis on an emotional process, a working over of material—a brooding—that results in unexpected articulation; this is a process strikingly similar to the processes of mourning that her characters engage in the Manawaka fiction.

As Laurence's protagonists attest, the time when the work of mourning needs to be performed most urgently is frequently far removed from the actual moment of loss. She depicts the periods when this work occurs as liminal in constitution, closely linking the shift from one state of existence to another with renewed and unresolved grief. Bowlby's theory that grief can return intermittently, catalyzed by life events, is particularly applicable to the mourning situations of Laurence's characters.[29] The pattern of Laurence's mourning protagonists is most accurately described when Bowlby's notions of the recurrence of grief and the necessary psychic reorganization to console that loss are combined with the concept of liminality—or, as Tolchin calls it, "the condition of being betwixt and between"[30] periods of a life. This concept was first developed by the social anthropologist Arnold van Gennep in 1909 in his book *The Rites of Passage*, and then later refined by another social anthropologist, Victor Turner.[31] Each of Laurence's protagonists finds herself in an untenable situation whereby her life is thrown off balance by a crisis that brings to immediacy a death or serious loss from the past, along with the attendant emotions. These characters can be considered to be in a liminal state where they cannot effectively move on with their lives without revisiting the past and working through the grief that plagues them. Loss initiates the need to move from one stage of life to another, and the work of mourning becomes the means for the protagonists to negotiate the emotional turmoil and the social and cultural codes that condition grief.

Van Gennep was interested in the "patterns which accompany a passage from one situation to another"[32]—what he described as transitional moments in an individual's life. Accompanying these moments of transition is a series of rites of passage.[33] He argued that rites of passage accompany most major developments in an individual's life, such as, for example, pregnancy and childbirth, childhood, initiation into adulthood, betrothal and marriage (the period of the engagement is an excellent example of a liminal moment), and funerals. His concept of the liminal state—the moment in a transitional period where the individual is literally in-between two states—can define the depiction of the protagonists in such a state of change.

Social psychologist Jill G. Morawski argues that "Liminality is the threshold, the betwixt and between of established social states," and that this "betwixt-and-between state . . . furnishes a place not just for momentary inversion, or reversal, of mundane social reality, but also for its ultimate subversion, or replacement."[34] Victor Turner states that "the most characteristic midliminal symbolism is that of paradox, or being *both* this and that."[35] In other words, the liminal space is one where new ways of proceeding, of relating to a life, are enacted so that they may affect everyday life.[36]

Laurence's descriptions of the situations of her characters and her use of language frequently reinforce liminal elements. The paradox presented in the opening line of *The Diviners*, for example, underscores the association of Morag Gunn to a liminal moment: "The river flowed both ways" (11). Elsewhere in the novel, when Morag is at Christie's funeral, she thinks of life by quoting Hamlet. "To be or not to be," she thinks, "that sure as death is the question" (326). To live, for Morag, is to grapple with the "two-way battle in the mindfield, the

minefield of the mind" (326). The idea of the mind as a bat-
tlefield of paradox is important for it reflects upon the oppositional forces of the work of mourning and reinforces the
necessity to labour at grief—to, in fact, labour against the
paradoxes that define the liminal. The process of the labour of
mourning asserts that being both this and that, to echo
Turner, is not a tenable position. Similarly, when Rachel
Cameron, in *A Jest of God*, realizes that it is wrong to see her
father, and his alcoholism, as a victim of life's circumstances,
she realizes that her situation is fraught with paradox: "If it is
true he wanted that life the most, why mourn? Why ever cease
from mourning?" Morag's thoughts about the river's flow as
an "impossible contradiction" (11) are apt for they accurately
describe the situations that all the protagonists face as their
worlds are destabilized by loss.

Victor Turner, in his extension of van Gennep, theorized
the movement through liminal states as being "dramatic,"
making the application of liminality to mourning all the more
convincing. The work of mourning is ultimately an active one,
and this work is performed by Laurence's characters in an act
of articulating the emotions of loss. This moment of articulation is what then allows the final move through and out of the
liminal stage. Mourning, work, and liminality all partake of
the process of articulating loss, which, in turn, is tantamount
to recognizing it and thus allows a necessary revaluation of the
self to occur in Laurence's protagonists. Bowlby's four phases
of mourning—numbing, yearning and searching for the lost
figure, disorganization and despair, and reorganization—help
to delineate the mourning work. The first two phases are rel-
atively brief, although individually variable, lasting from a few
hours to a week in the first phase and from a few months to a
few years in the second, and are generally not applicable to the
stages of grief that Laurence depicts in her characters.[37] The
third and fourth phases can be of much longer duration and

are most applicable to Laurence's protagonists.[38] Tolchin suggests that what van Gennep terms "incorporation"—the postliminal stage—and what Turner termed "reintegration" is similar to Bowlby's assertion that the "process of grief generates a renewed sense of reorganization"[39] and that in the mourner this reorganization "entails a redefinition of himself as well as of his situation."[40] Bowlby further elucidates this theme by pointing out that "this redefinition of self and situation is as painful as it is crucial, if only because it means relinquishing finally all hope that the lost person can be recovered and the old situation re-established. Yet until redefinition is achieved no plans for the future can be made."[41] Philosopher and death counsellor Thomas Attig echoes Bowlby by terming the reorganization "relearning the world" and states that "relearning our selves and the patterns of caring that define us as individuals is tantamount to reintegrating our selves."[42]

Although Margaret Laurence wrote two other important books of adult fiction, *The Tomorrow-Tamer* (1958) and *This Side Jordan* (1960), both set in Africa, as well as other significant non-fictional and children's books, her five works of fiction set in Manawaka (a fictional rendition of her hometown of Neepawa, Manitoba) represent a thematically unified conception of the work of mourning as it pertains to a wide range of women living in Canada: an old and dying woman, a spinster schoolteacher, a middle-aged housewife, and two writers. Each novel, in order of publication date, reflects the development of Laurence's interest in exploring her protagonists' movement towards articulation in their work of mourning. The Manawaka fiction cannot be defined as a progression of sophistication in Laurence's conception of the work of mourning; the progression occurs at the level of self-consciousness in her characters in relation to the articulation of mourning. The

first three novels examine the protagonists' gradual awareness—hence self-consciousness—of their work of mourning,
and the last two explore in greater detail the self-conscious
mourner creating a textual work, fully aware of its resonances
in terms of her emotions.

In her first novel set in Manawaka, *The Stone Angel*,
Laurence depicts the last weeks, days, and moments of an old
woman named Hagar Shipley. Hagar encounters the multiple
problems of facing her own impending death and of suffering
from the lingering feelings of unresolved grief in relation to
the deaths of her husband Bram and her son John. Laurence
charts her protagonist's struggle to mourn her lost men, and
then herself, as a three-part liminal movement. In the first,
Hagar resists the signs of her physical decline, and, by doing
so, resists her own mortality. Unprepared for death, she is also
not ready to mourn herself. The second movement, depicted
in Hagar's departure from home for Shadow Point, marks the
first step in her active work of mourning. As this movement
progresses, she becomes increasingly aware of her physical
deterioration, and, through the intervention of a passing
stranger, she is able to perform the work of mourning in relation to both Bram and John. Having resolved this grief from
the past, Hagar is prepared for the third and final liminal
movement—the one that ends only with her own death. Her
world now restricted to the hospital, Hagar focusses on her *self*
and the one remaining familial connection, her son Marvin.
Her work of mourning here is fully self-conscious and allows
her peace before death, as well as providing a positive legacy
for Marvin.

In *A Jest of God* the focus is on Rachel Cameron, the stereotyped small-town spinster schoolteacher. When the novel
opens, Rachel is trapped in a static world shadowed by her
father's untimely death fourteen years earlier, just as she was
making her independent place in the world. Rachel must

learn to mourn her father effectively, despite social and cultural strictures that define mourning as a taboo. Her work of mourning is performed over the course of the novel, beginning with two moments where she breaks taboos, in the Tabernacle with Calla and then in her sexual experiences with Nick, that then prepare her to confront the familial and social taboo against mourning. She makes tenuous steps forward while continuing to face obstacles to effective resolution. When, finally, she believes herself pregnant, she is forced to choose life or death, and, thus, must concede the effects of grief on her life. The result is that she self-consciously performs the most difficult elements of her work of mourning.

Stacey, Rachel's sister and the protagonist of *The Fire-Dwellers*, feels constricted by her life of domesticity, as well as by the larger world around her. Stacey feels trapped in her life, stuck in a liminal state, unsure of how to extricate herself. The personal and cosmic duality of her constriction defines Stacey's mourning, for she grieves her lost youth, the loss of happiness in her marriage, her lost family, and the failure of her own dreams of personal happiness, as well as the failure of the contemporary world to offer meaning. Laurence delineates Stacey's struggles to find ways to mourn the state of her life, and presents her work of mourning as haphazard. Her work of mourning is marked by a series of experiences of otherness that she seeks out in reaction to her emotional unease. While her work of mourning is primarily reactive, it is clear that Stacey feels compelled to seek out these experiences. It is not primarily a consciously *worked-at* effort, but it is impelled by a deeper psychic need.

The final two books, *A Bird in the House* and *The Diviners*, are Laurence's exploration of the textual and aesthetic articulation of the work of mourning. The characters' means of grieving becomes the active creation of a work of mourning—a creative text that, by its articulation, enables psychic reparation. The activity of writing itself fulfills the work of mourning, and the resulting text becomes an artefact of that grieving (or a "work" of mourning). For Vanessa in *A Bird in the House* and Morag in *The Diviners*, the work of mourning moves them through the state of liminality that is precipitated by loss. Vanessa revisits her parents' graves and her grandfather's house—which stands as his monument— many years after having last seen them, and her grief is reawakened. The stories she tells, the ones we read, become her work of mourning through the process of telling them. In *The Diviners*, Morag Gunn is a writer for whom the act of textual production is a mode of reacting to and coping with the world around her. In the novel, the feelings of loss at her parents' deaths when she was a child are reawakened by her daughter's sudden departure; Morag composes a novel that is structured around the four significant instances of death in her life, as the means to understand her ancestral history and its continuing effects on her life. *The Diviners* takes the form of what I term the *thanatosroman*, a variant on the *künstlerroman*. In the *thanatosroman*, the development of the artist is linked with experiences of death that have affected the main character.

As a sequence, the Manawaka novels represent an idealized aesthetic enterprise for Laurence, as she asserts the power of language to signify and to ultimately bring about emotional change. Language *means* in these books, and articulating pain and loss is an emotionally significant and satisfying endeavour. The process of unearthing the past, and confronting loss, however chaotically, is ultimately positive for the protagonists, inspiring them with hope for the future. Laurence asserts the power of performing the work of mourning in guiding the individual through a potentially perpetual liminal state, despite the difficulties involved in overcoming the psychic disruptions caused by loss.

Laurence demonstrates her sophisticated understanding of the complexity of mourning in the mid- to late twentieth century in her Manawaka fiction. The work of mourning is posited as a process that must be carried out as a private activity, for the world her protagonists occupy constrains its performance and challenges its legitimacy. Thus, the five novels that form the basis of this study proclaim the beneficial possibilities of the work of mourning and serve as models of hope for her readers.

CHAPTER ONE

SPEAKING THE HEART'S TRUTH:
HAGAR'S WORK OF MOURNING IN
THE STONE ANGEL

"When did I ever speak the heart's truth?"

With *The Stone Angel* Margaret Laurence begins her exploration of the psychic changes of the mourning subject that continues through four more novels. In this novel she chooses the difficult task of depicting the final weeks, days, and, ultimately, moments of her protagonist's long life, and the complex mental responses that occur when a person becomes increasingly aware of her incipient demise. Complicating Hagar's reaction to her impending death is her slow move toward self-consciousness about her fate, and, thus, she only comes to a greater understanding of her life, and to fully mourn her death, in the final chapters of the novel. Laurence's protagonist subconsciously resists the failure of her body at first, then gradually becomes more aware of her failing health, before finally coming to an uneasy acceptance of her death.

Laurence's focus on this movement to self-consciousness prefigures her central concern with grieving in the four other Manawaka books, for Hagar's work of mourning encompasses attributes of the other protagonists and their work. Hagar's initial resistance toward mourning is akin to Rachel's and Stacey's attempts at denying their grief—and their need to work through it—and her slow move to acceptance of, and then working through, her grief is similar to their journeys of awareness. When she becomes fully self-conscious of her mourning at the end of the novel, however, Hagar is more like Vanessa and Morag as they consciously and actively work through, and repair, loss.

Hagar's passage to the final moments of her life is figured as an increasingly self-consciously liminal one and as the final liminal stage of a lifetime. Her story begins with the prevalence of the symptoms of her physical decline, but it is only when she accepts the consequences of those signs that she is fully free to come to terms with the loss of her own life. Central to her liminal stage is the work of mourning that Hagar performs in preparation for death and that allows her to delve deep into the repressed emotions of loss so that she can "speak the heart's truth" (292). The novel is divided into three movements that correspond to the development of her work of mourning, which is depicted as a three-level liminal stage. The first movement marks Hagar's resistance to her declining health and signals her entry into liminality; the second presents her increasing awareness of her decline and represents her active and self-conscious mourning of the losses of her husband and son; and the final movement demonstrates her acceptance of, and final preparations for, her impending death, which also inevitably marks the end of her liminal stage.

A number of critics have noted Hagar's attempts to understand her life retrospectively so that she can find meaning in the many events of her past that still affect her in the present. Jon Kertzer remarks in *"The Stone Angel:* Time and Responsibility," "Through memory, Hagar relives her life in order to understand and come to terms with it. . . . Now in retrospect, Hagar must sum herself up, tie her life together. She must reconcile the different periods in her life in order to find coherence and hence meaning in it."[1] The role of the work of mourning in Hagar's move towards her own death, however, has not yet been examined: mourning is integral to understanding Hagar's need to revisit the past as her own present moves ever closer to its inevitable end.

The opening sections of *The Stone Angel* depict Hagar's resistance to the degeneration of her body and her denial of that failure of the flesh. Throughout the four chapters Hagar is made aware of her body's decline, and her memory sequences implicitly and subtly reinforce her physical strength: she is the survivor, while the main figures she remembers died prematurely as a consequence of their physical weaknesses. Hagar's father is significant in her memories too, but he is figured as a symbol of strength. He is *living* proof of the power of physical and mental strength, and, thus, his certainty in all matters is implicitly signalled as a quality worth emulating. As James King remarks, "from an early age, Hagar's identity is shaped by her father" (161). In all these sequences, memory becomes a reinforcing agent of Hagar's strength.

Laurence also establishes in the opening pages of the novel that Hagar has not accorded herself, to employ Derrida's phrase, the right to mourn the loss of her husband Bram and youngest son John. As Hagar states, "Oh my lost men. No, I will not think of that. What a disgrace to be seen crying by that fat Doris" (6). The linking of shame and grief is important as it reinforces the difficulty with which Hagar will engage in the work of mourning. Further, the disgrace of crying indicates the shame of externalizing emotions, which is paradigmatic of the experiences of Laurence's four other protagonists in the remaining novels in the Manawaka series.

Signs of Hagar's physical decline are shown early in the novel when she is troubled by her increasing dependency, caused by her aging, on her son Marvin and his wife Doris, but she shows no acknowledgement that their involvement in her daily life is a specific sign of her physical decline. She is upset that "The door of my room has no lock. They say it is because I might get taken ill in the night, and then how could they get in to tend me (*tend*—as though I were a crop, a cash crop). So they may enter my room at any time they choose. Privacy is a privilege not granted to the aged" (6). Here, Hagar interprets the cause of this invasion of her life as age and not health, demonstrating her denial of her deteriorating body. It is common, she reasons, for the aged and "very young children" to have their humanity denied by "the middling ones" (6). Thus, she feels misunderstood as a stereotyped, frail, old woman by Marvin and Doris because of her age and elides the effects of her deteriorating health.

Nonetheless, her physical instability is impossible to ignore, despite her best efforts. In one scene with Doris, she falls, and "The pain under my ribs is the worst, the one that has been coming more frequently of late, although I have mentioned nothing of it to Marvin or Doris" (31). She realizes she is getting sicker, but it is, in fact, her incapacity that contributes most to her crisis and her recognition of it: "The pain burns through to my heart and I cannot breathe for a moment. I gasp and flounder like a fish on the slimed boards of a dock" (31). At the same time, she resists identifying herself as the weak one: "'Leave me, leave me—' Can this torn voice be mine? A series of yelps, like an injured dog" (31). The simile reinforces her psychic sense of distance from her failing body's alien sounds, for she does not imagine herself as an old, dying woman, but as an animal. A short time later, Hagar feels further signs of the seriousness of her undiagnosed illness: "I cannot speak, for the pain under my ribs returns now, all of a stab. Lungs, is it? Heart? This pain is hot, hot as August rain or the tears of children" (35). The pain accompanies Marvin's and Doris's suggestion that Hagar's house be sold because it is too large. In a sad irony, Hagar, who always finds it hard holding back her words, is silenced now by her body's weakness.

The signs of Hagar's physical frailty are countered by her memories of her mother—beginning with the opening scene of *The Stone Angel*—and brothers, who died prematurely. Hagar's focus on, and then active remembering of, their deaths is a sign of her own fear of her body's decline into illness and then, ultimately, into death. We see, in her remembrance of the death scenes,[2] no overt mourning on her part. She does not grieve the losses particularly. The deaths she still acutely feels (Bram's and John's), she pushes aside. Thus, the conscious return to the deaths functions as a more deeply originated statement of her fear of her own decline, and the memories become oppositional markers of her strength.

The novel opens with the scene of the stone angel that marks her mother's gravesite, but that is also a marker of physical weakness, in Hagar's view. James King states that "[Hagar] can only conceive of her mother as the antithesis of her self."[3] Critic Michel Fabré notes that "the Angel is dedicated to her mother, but she is weak, quasi-nonexistent in life as in death."[4] Another critic, Alice Bell, remarks that, "For Hagar, the stone angels in the Manawaka cemetery are symbols of passive weak-spirited women who acquiesced with death because they did not have the strength to deal with life."[5] While the angel ostensibly memorializes her mother, the literal purpose of the angel is primarily a function of Hagar's father's patriarchal tendencies, for it was "bought in pride to mark her bones and proclaim his dynasty, as he fancied, forever and a day" (3).[6]

The memory of the angel is not presented as a wistful long-ing for the mother's return, in Hagar's mind, for the angel is depicted with weak attributes, reflecting the person it marks: "[S]he viewed the town with sightless eyes. She was doubly blind, not only stone but unendowed with even a pretense of sight. Whoever carved her had left the eyeballs blank. ... Her wings in winter were pitted by the snow and in summer by the blown grit" (3). Significantly, while the description of the stone angel is detailed, an equally elaborate account is pre-sented of another stone angel in the graveyard that commem-orates Regina Weese,[7] who, Hagar thinks, "had only herself to blame [for her death], for she was a flimsy, gutless creature" (4). A physically weak person, Hagar implies, deserves an early death. Hagar remembers her mother in similar terms to Regina, for, in her words, her mother "relinquished her feeble ghost" (3).[8]

The pattern of Hagar's remembering in the next sequences is set in this opening scene, for Hagar's returns to scenes from the past that depict weak family members are frequent, and all are figured with her mother's attributes. When she thinks of her brothers, she considers that they "took after our mother, graceful unspirited boys" (7-8). She considers her brother Dan's weakness in relation to the mother when he is on his deathbed—"all I could think of was that meek woman I'd never seen, the woman Dan was said to resemble so much and from whom he'd inherited a frailty I could not help detest" (25)—and she is unable to console him when Matt asks her to wear their mother's shawl to comfort Dan: "To play at being her—it was beyond me" (25). In being "unable to bend enough" (25), Hagar reinforces the origin of her dislike for physical weakness, in her mother's frail body, but a further explanation for her inability to accept her present decline is signalled: Hagar is conditioned from youth to an aversion to the physically weak that supercedes conscious rationality by her father's favouring her because she "was sturdy like him" (8). Just as she was "unable to bend enough" to console Dan, she is now unable to recognize and accept her own weakness.

When Hagar learns of Matt's death, she has a similar reaction of abhorrence to the seemingly facile manner with which he gave up his life. Aunt Dolly, the housekeeper, tells Hagar that "he went quietly. . . . he didn't fight his death, as some do. They only make it harder for themselves. Matt seemed to know there was no help for it. . . . He didn't struggle to breathe, or try to hang on. He let himself slip away" (60). Hagar's response is indicative of her reaction to her own decline in the present of the narrative: "I found this harder to bear than his death, even. Why hadn't he writhed, cursed, at least grappled with the thing?" (60). Matt's passivity is, in fact, the antithesis of the way she approaches the signs of her demise, for Hagar fights and struggles as long as possible.

The origin of her siblings' weakness, in Hagar's eyes, as we have seen, is the mother, and Hagar is clear in her depiction of her—a figuring that borders on the contemptuous. In a long passage, Hagar considers a "daguerreotype of her" that her father gave her "when I was a child" (59). In this sequence, Hagar is clearly "reading" the photo, imbuing it with meaning, although she does not do so self-reflexively. She views her mother as "a spindly and anxious girl," clearly figuring her as weak. Further, Hagar denounces her mother's anxiety: "She looks so worried that she will not know what to do, although she came of good family and ought not have had a moment's hesitation about the propriety of her ways" (59). Hagar is clearly troubled by this vision of her "perplexed" mother, especially as her mother died during the birth of her third child: "and even then it seemed so puzzling to me that she'd not died when either of the boys was born, but saved her death for me" (59). Hagar recognizes she is quite opposite to her mother's characteristics: "I used to wonder what she'd been like, that docile woman, and wonder at her weakness and my awful strength" (59). That recognition adds another level of signification to the scene, building on the pattern of Hagar's remembering. The weak mother has died in order to give life to the strong daughter, and the act of remembering the scene reinforces in Hagar the belief in her own physical strength. These reminiscences, then, remind Hagar of her strength. She was strong in the past, as her memories attest, and now, when she is showing to others clear signs of decline, these memories will help assure her of her continuing robustness and underscore her resistance to the work of mourning.

As the first movement of the novel progresses, however, it becomes more difficult for memory to overcome the obvious physical signs of Hagar's decline. While she does not completely acknowledge the marks of her impending end, she does begin to distinguish them more clearly. Hagar recognizes a harbinger of her decline, despite being horrified, when she accidentally sees the ad from the newspaper lying open on the kitchen table: "It is then that I see the newspaper and the dreadful words" (53):

> *Only the Best Will Do*
> *for*
> *Mother*

Do you find it impossible to give Mother the specialized care she needs in her declining years? SILVER THREADS Nursing Home provides skilled care for Senior Citizens. Here in the pleasant cozy atmosphere of our Lodge, Mother will find the companionship of Qualified medical staff. Reasonable terms. Why wait until it is too late? (53-4)

Hagar responds by paying attention to the particularities of her body, which she now defines as a body in decline. Indeed,

she figures her body in corpse-like terms and echoes the
phrases of the most common funeral rites:

> [M]y hands are dry and quiet. . . . My throat, too, is dry,
> and my mouth. As I brush my fingers over my own wrist,
> the skin seems too white after the sunburned years, and
> too dry, powdery as blown dust when the rains failed,
> flaking with dryness as an old bone will flake and chalk,
> left out in the sun that grinds bone and flesh and earth to
> dust as though in a mortar of fire with a pestle of crush-
> ing light. (54)

Hagar echoes the familiar funeral rites: "Dust to dust / Ashes
to ashes." Her reaction to the ad is physical, opposing the previous mental responses: "Up flames the pain now, and I am
speared once more, the blade driving under my ribs. . . . Breath
goes" (54). And again, she fears death: "Can a body hold to
this life more than an instant with empty lungs?" (54).

A second look at her image a short time later reinforces her
recognition of her declining body, despite her protestations to
the contrary: "I'm only preparing against the day. But it won't
be for a while yet, I can promise you that" (65). She sees herself as a grotesque, inhuman creature with a face beyond hope
of reparation:

> I . . . see a puffed face purpled with veins as though some-
> one had scribbled over the skin with an indelible pencil.
> The skin itself is the silverish white of the creatures one
> fancies must live under the sea where the sun never
> reaches. Below the eyes the shadows bloom as though
> two soft black petals had been stuck there. The hair
> which should by rights be black is yellowed white, like
> damask stored too long in a damp basement. (79)

This is the face of a person of considerable age, the marks
of a lifetime making themselves evident. Her physical self is
clearly prepared for the final movement to death, but Hagar's

mental self still resists what is told in the image reflected back to her.

The unexpected trip to Silver Threads, after Doris and Marvin trick her into going, is for Hagar another harbinger of her end, for she feels that if she acquiesces to their request that she stay there, she will be acknowledging her decline openly and, thus, making it real. Here again, Hagar is unable to resist physically, reinforcing the belief that she is becoming unsound: she is "overcome with fear, the feeling one has when the ether mask goes on, when the mind cries out to the limbs, *'flail against the thing*,' but the limbs are already touched with lethargy, bound and lost" (95), similar to her brother Matt. The mind is still willing to resist, but the body is failing miserably, and no mental gymnastics will allow Hagar to escape from the reality of her situation.

The increasing knowledge of her own impending death causes old losses, over which she is still conflicted, to resurface for Hagar. She lies about John's death in her conversation with one of the old ladies at the home: "'Two sons.' Then I realize what I've said. 'I mean, I had two. One was killed—in the last war'. . . . I wonder why I've said that, especially as it doesn't happen to be true" (104). This uncontrolled speech is a sign of the kind of psychic space that the visit to Silver Threads occasions, for further troubled memories come forth soon thereafter. Hagar is troubled and confused by her physical failing, and in that state her mind is less guarded about the losses of the past. This is attested when she mistakes a man in the garden for Bram, for in this scene she loses touch with reality and no longer knows if she is dead or alive:

> Although his face is hidden, I can see his beard. Oh—
> So familiar he is that I cannot move nor speak nor breathe. How has he come here, by what mystery? Or have I come to the place he went before? This is a strange place, surely, shadowed and luminous, the trees

enfolding us like arms in the sheltering dark. If I speak to
him, slowly, so as not to startle, will he turn to me with
such a look of recognition that I hardly dare hope for it,
and speak my name? (105-06)

The old man, of course, is not Bram reincarnated nor is Hagar
dead, though she appears not completely surprised by this
possibility. Significantly, however, Hagar's increasing thoughts
of her own demise have brought old emotions to the fore, and,
when Doris finds her, Hagar is crying. The release of emotion
signals Hagar's increased readiness to face the losses of the
past, although several further steps are necessary before she
can fully mourn those losses.

Liminal signs accompany Hagar's perception of her declining health, and her recognition of them as such indicates her
growing awareness of impending and inevitable change. As
she undergoes a complicated x-ray, where she has to wait,
strapped to a machine, she compares her current predicament
to her marriage with Bram: "I've waited like this, for things to
get better or worse, many and many a time, I should be used
to it" (112). While she is literally waiting for the x-ray, the
metaphorical overtones of the scene are obvious to narrator
and reader, for Hagar realizes she is waiting for more than the
medical process to be completed. This sense of waiting for
something to happen—better or worse health, or perhaps
even death—is reinforced a few pages later when she looks up
at the clouds and imagines herself much younger: "How I
shall hate to go away for good" (120). Finally, Hagar explicitly
acknowledges that the signs of her ill health are penetrating
her consciousness, and that knowledge prepares her for the
next stage of liminality. She is not yet ready to concede her
impending death, but she does lament that her failing health
is having an effect on her daily life.

The second movement of Hagar's work of mourning begins
with the shift into the next level of her liminal stage, for she is

31

now no longer able to ignore her poor health. This shift is marked by her memory of her leave-taking from Manawaka when life with Bram had become too much, and it sets the scene for her own departure from home: "Each venture and launching is impossible until it becomes necessary, and then there's a way, and it doesn't do to be too fussy about the means" (135). Shortly after this memory, Hagar is faced with her distasteful future in the nursing home, and she makes a decision to leave: "Revelations are saved for times of actual need, and now one comes to me" (139). The designation of her current situation as a time of "need" is significant here, as is her decision to make her own way as she did so many years before. Thus, the trip to Shadow Point she then embarks upon becomes a re-enactment of past departures. She envisions herself in a "new house" at the cannery, and imagines herself starting over again. The name of the place she goes to symbolically reflects the nature of her journey, for it is there that she most closely examines the "shadows" from her past: the deaths of Bram and John. This is the most important movement in her work of mourning as Hagar becomes self-conscious about the liminal mode she is in and where she makes overt links between her memories and her current crisis. While the final movement of the liminal stage leads to her death, and her acceptance of that passing, it is the second movement that allows the "positive" end to her life.

Hagar hatches the plan all on her own, yet her diminished physical condition makes her reliant on others to execute it: Doris must help her with her clothes in the morning; the bus driver helps her to the bus depot; a young girl shows her where the ticket window is; and another person helps her to the bus. When she finally arrives at the turnoff to Shadow Point, Hagar forgets the shopping bag of supplies in the store and must be chased after, and she is given a ride by a passing motorist for the final three miles. Her previous departures, from her father's house and then from Bram's house, were self-reliant and marked key moments of independence;[9] thus, her diminished physical ability becomes a signal to her of the impossibility of once again making her life anew. Nonetheless, she makes a valiant attempt at it.

The place that Hagar has chosen for her new life appears to her as an elemental place, or a place that is slowly returning to its pre-human contact state: "I'm standing among trees that extend all the way down the steep slopes to the sea. How quiet the forest is, only its own voices, no human noises at all" (150). And when she descends the hill to the cannery, the signs of natural dominance persist: "The stairway's beginning is almost concealed by fern and bracken. ... It's not a proper stairway, actually. The steps have been notched into the hillside" (151). For Hagar, the scene is conducive to self-conscious rumination about the past—and, ultimately, to self-conscious mourning of past losses. The descent to the cannery, then, has the air of a physical enactment of her psychological descent to the secrets that haunt her subconscious. Once there, the work of mourning in all its difficulty commences in earnest for her.

The first building she comes to at the bottom of the stairs is a small house that symbolically beckons her to enter: "A door's ajar. I push it and walk in. ... I hunch down in the dust and go to sleep" (152). After she awakens, it is as if she has awakened to a psychic space that most approximates a liminal space: "One day at a time—that's all a person has to deal with. I'll not look ahead" (153). The references to liminal thoughts are numerous, and her conscious consideration of them is important to her impending work of mourning, for she feels ready and willing to embrace change in her life. "To move to a new place," she thinks, "that's the greatest excitement. For a while you believe you carry nothing with you—all is canceled from before, or cauterized, and you begin again and nothing will go wrong this time" (155).

She revisits the move to Vancouver and the starting over with John, which was also a liminal movement for her: "It was a becalmed life we led there, a period of waiting and of marking time. But the events we waited for, unknowingly, turned out to be quite other than what I imagined they might be" (160). The conscious links to her present crisis are obvious: "And here I am, the same Hagar, in a different establishment once more, and waiting again" (160).

This time, Hagar's experience is marked by her illness and her aging, as the return of her pain reinforces: "Under my ribs the soreness spreads" (162). She then shows signs of confusion—"I wonder now if I am here at all, or if I only imagine myself to be" (162)—becoming bewildered about where she is. She thinks Marvin and Doris have left her behind: "Every last one of them has gone away and left me. I never left them. It was the other way around, I swear it" (164). In this state of delirium, Hagar's remembrance of John's return to Manawaka and Bram's death is enabled. In a sense, her defenses are now down, due to her illness and mental state, helping her to dredge up the old losses she has so far refused to mourn.

The return to the memory of Bram's death is a reminder to Hagar of her inability to mourn him. She notes his indifference to her in his last days, and she struggles to understand John's devotion to, and grief for, Bram. When she returns to Manawaka because Bram is dying, he does not even recognize her: "He didn't know me. He didn't speak my name. He didn't say a word" (172). When he does recognize her, he tells her that she reminds him of "his fat and cow-like first wife" (173). Hagar feels as if she has been erased from his life, and the years she spent with him in rebellion against her father become meaningless. Thus, she constructs her inability to mourn him when he has died as a consequence of Bram's lack of regard for her: "[W]hen we'd buried Bram and come home again and lighted the lamps for the evening, it was John who cried, not I" (184). While there was an immediate failure to mourn Bram, the rehearsal of the death scene in the present has a cathartic effect on her, for she admits to his influence upon her: "I know I'd nagged at him in the past, but God knows I'd had my reasons. And yet he'd mattered to me" (184). Here, Hagar admits her inability to mourn Bram, and, in doing this apparently simple act, she effectively allows a moment of honesty in respect to his influence over her. He *did* matter to her, she realizes, despite her denial of that fact for so many years. In an implicit acknowledgement of his influence over her, several pages later, when she is in the forest and has fallen down, she speaks in Bram's discourse: "I grow enraged. I curse like Bram, summoning every blasphemy I can lay my hands on" (191). And these words then give her the strength to extricate herself from her difficult situation: "Perhaps the anger gives me strength, for I clutch at a bough, not caring if it's covered with pins and needles or not, and yank myself upright" (191). Her discursive act here re-enacts her rebellion from her father so many years ago and denotes her independence.

Having rehearsed Bram's death, and having acknowledged an influence on her life heretofore suppressed, Hagar is psychically enabled to examine the other death that haunts her so: John's death. Hagar moves from the house to the cannery for this exploration. The cannery is figured by her as a place of fragments or residues: "A place of remnants and oddities, this seems, more like a sea-chest of some old and giant sailor than merely a cannery no one has used for years" (215). And again, a metaphorical reading is appropriate here, for this is the place where Hagar dredges up remnants of old loss and explores their significance to her life. Like the initial descent to the cannery on the previous day, this place is depicted as a slightly magical or mystical spot. Contributing to this sense of strangeness for Hagar is the fact that she has difficulty grasping reality. As she notes, "I can't recall exactly what I did this morning. . . . Perhaps I cleaned that other house. I can't abide a messy house" (217). In this place she is in a state of confusion, and it is this confusion, amplified by the intervention of Murray F. Lees and his alcohol, that is the final catalyst for Hagar's deep-rooted work of mourning in relation to John to be performed. It is notable that Hagar's feelings of loss are so deeply repressed that such drastic conditions are needed for the emotions to be released. She remembers that "The night my son died I was transformed to stone and never wept at all" (243), and it is this rock that must be, and is, shattered in this sequence.

The story of his own son's death that Lees tells catalyzes Hagar's revisitation of John's death. Hagar learns from Lees that allowing grief its expression can be beneficial, and, further, she commiserates with him about his loss, for they are in a sense as equals in this case, despite their vast differences. When Hagar attempts to console Lees, she is left not knowing what to say: "I can tell him nothing. I can think of only one thing to say with any meaning. 'I had a son,' I say, 'and lost him'" (234). That seemingly simple statement involves no emotional exchange between the two, but it does confirm a similarity of experience of loss, and that, as Lees confirms, is enough to bring them together: "'Well,' he says abruptly, 'then you know'" (234). This parallel of experience is what allows Hagar to tell the story of John's death and allows her involvement with it to occur soon thereafter. While Hagar is unaware that she is speaking aloud, the action of articulating her grief is integral to her understanding of her son's death.

Murray prompts her in her telling and brings the hitherto repressed emotion to the fore. Hagar remembers suppressing her tears in the hospital after John died: "I wouldn't cry in front of strangers, whatever it cost me" (242). But, after telling her story, she is "crying now, I think. I put a hand to my face, and find the skin slippery with my tears" (244). Murray's role in bringing Hagar's emotions to the fore, and her resistance to that experience, is clear when she thinks, "I didn't mean to tell him this" (245). After a short contemplation, however, Hagar realizes the consolatory power of the encounter: "I'm not sorry I've talked to him, not sorry at all, and that's remarkable" (245). While she still does not "accept it," and "It angers me, and will until I die" (245), Lees's words of understanding bring her some release and are what allow her to find some peace in relation to John's death. "I know what you mean" (245), says Lees in response to Hagar's lament for the "senseless" and "pointless" nature of John's death.

The most important moment in Hagar's work of mourning in relation to John comes when she awakens and believes she is addressing him with her apology: "I didn't mean it, about not bringing her here. A person speaks in haste. I've always had a temper."[10] The enaction of the apology becomes the performance of Hagar's work of mourning, for it is here that she can hope for the weight of guilt to be lifted, as she notes: "I've spoken so calmly, so reasonably. He can't in all conscience refuse what I've said" (247). Murray allows Hagar consolation by playing the role of John, and in doing so permits the performance of the work of mourning to continue: "It's okay. . . . I knew all the time you never meant it. Everything is all right. You try to sleep. Everything's quite okay" (248). "I sigh, content" (248), Hagar says. Her guilt has now been alleviated.

The next morning Hagar has dim memories of the work of mourning that took place. As she notes, "Something else occurred last night. Some other words were spoken, words which I've forgotten and cannot for the life of me recall. But why do I feel bereaved as though I'd lost someone recently?" (249). The feeling of bereavement is central to Hagar's experience, as she denied herself that emotional response so many years ago. Having enacted grief through a renewal of the emotions of loss, she realizes she was somehow able to work through the complexities of John's death: "I am left with the feeling that it was a kind of mercy I encountered [Murray], even though this gain is mingled mysteriously with the sense of loss I felt earlier this morning" (253). Freedom from loss's strong hold on Hagar need not be at a fully conscious level, just as her repressed grief was not self-consciously enacted. The key, then, to understanding these passages is to recognize that Hagar has acknowledged the emotions of loss. This acquiescence frees Hagar to mourn her own impending death, and she can now enter into her own final liminal movement.

The arrival of Marvin and Doris to rescue Hagar from Shadow Point marks the beginning of the final movement of her liminal stage. The signs of her physical decline are now completely undeniable to Hagar, and, while that recognition is in itself not a sign of her preparedness for death, her freedom from the haunting losses of the past allows her to focus her attention more fully on herself and her soon-to-be survivors. In this movement, she comes to a final transformative moment where the body is laid waste, but psychically she demonstrates her readiness for the end of her life.

The third movement begins with the signs of Hagar's physical weakness when she describes herself as no longer able to resist the actions of others: "I lie there huge and immovable, like an old hawk caught, eyes wide open, unblinking" (252). When Marvin questions Lees's account of his involvement with Hagar, she once again becomes aware of her body's decline: "I feel a mute gratitude toward Marvin. He's not easily taken in. In my heart I have to admit I'm relieved to see him. Yet I despise my gladness. Have I grown so weak I must rejoice at being captured, taken alive?" (252). This deferral designates the pattern of Hagar's interaction with others from here on, for she must rely on them for the most basic of activities. Ascending the stairs, for example, becomes a struggle whereby she must place all her weight, literal and symbolic, upon Marvin: "He tugs and pulls, sweats and strains, teeters me aloft. I'm dizzy, only half aware as we mount the steps, one and one and one, interminably. Marvin's arms are like a steel brace around me" (254). Hagar is now no longer the independent leader who chooses her own destiny, and the literal reliance upon Marvin becomes a symbolic passing on of her strength to him.

The strongest sign of Hagar's acceptance of her demise comes when she is told of her terminal illness. "Odd," she thinks. "Only now do I see that what's going to happen can't be delayed indefinitely" (254). Her lack of struggle at this news reinforces the positive effects of the work of mourning she completed at the cannery, for she is no longer troubled by the deaths of Bram and John. Her sole focus, now, is on her own death and her survivors. The limiting of her physical space—"Lord, how the world has shrunk. Now it's only one enormous room" (254)—parallels the narrowed internal concerns of the dying woman. The world has shrunk into insignificance, and only those who are still alive to enter into her metaphorical death room need attending to.

The hospital ward that Hagar occupies operates as a sort of Greek chorus, a community of voices that at first disturbs Hagar, but then comforts her. When Mrs. Jardine asks her about John, as Hagar spoke his name aloud in the night, she is initially upset, but then becomes accepting: "She means well, I suppose" (261). Rather than being troubled by her unconscious speech, and the references to the dead, Hagar is clearly accepting his death—thus further reinforcing her successful work of mourning in the previous movement. Several pages later, when the two are in conversation about their husbands, Hagar figures Bram in positive terms, showing no sign that his life and death still trouble her: "He was a big man. . . . Strong as a horse. He had a beard black as the ace of spades. He was a handsome man, a handsome man" (272).

As Hagar continues undeniably onwards towards her own death, she chooses to image her life in terms of limitations, conceding she will not return to the larger spaces occupied by the healthy. She considers the small size of the hospital room she is moved into: "The world is smaller now. It's shrinking now. It's shrinking so quickly" (282). She realizes, ironically, that there are no smaller rooms to be moved into during her lifetime: "The next room will be the smallest of all" (282). When Hagar voices this thought to the nurse, she is admonished about thinking in this way. Hagar, however, erases the shame associated with death, showing her own acceptance of her impending death: "An embarrassing subject, better not mentioned. The way we used to feel, when I was a girl, about undergarments or the two-backed beast of love. But I want to take hold of her arm, force her attention. *Listen. You must listen. It's—quite an event*" (282). This appeal to legitimize death as a matter that must be dealt with, recognized for what it is, opposes the many deaths Hagar elided in her life. Her refusal to mourn Bram, John, and even her mother is negated by her insistence on the value of her own death. The focus on event, with its overtones of celebration, reinforces the positive outlook Hagar now has towards her death.

The return of Reverend Troy catalyzes the transformative epiphany that allows Hagar to die with some degree of peace, but that also allows her to bestow that peace upon her son Marvin. Hagar asks Troy to sing a prayer that brings about her change. While it is the hymn itself that sparks the change, I want to underscore that it is the series of mourning events to date, cumulatively, that allows Hagar this moment of self-awareness. Troy sings:

> *All people that on earth do dwell,*
> *Sing to the Lord with joyful voice.*
> *Him serve with mirth, His praise forth tell;*
> *Come ye before Him and rejoice.* (291-92)

Hagar's response to the hymn is to recognize the oppositional power of the words, for she becomes fully conscious of how far from "joyfully" she lived her life: "Pride was my wilderness, and the demon that led me there was fear. I was alone, never anything else, and never free, for I carried my chains within me, and they spread out from me and shackled all I touched" (292). Troy's words become a reminder, a marker, of the gradual awareness she has been developing of her own temperament and its effect upon others over the long years of her life:

> This knowing comes upon me so forcefully, so shatter-ingly, and with such bitterness as I have never felt before. I must always, always, have wanted that—simply to rejoice. How is it I never could? I know, I know. How long have I known? Or have I always known, in some far crevice of my heart, some cave too deeply buried, too concealed? Every good joy I might have held, in my man or any child of mine or even the plain light of morning, of walking the earth, was forced to a standstill by some brake of proper appearances—oh, proper to whom? When did I ever speak the heart's truth? (292)

This passage echoes the literal descent into the cannery earlier in the novel, as well as the metaphorical revisitation of the past that occurred there. In the cannery, Hagar was able to delve into her mind to dig up the deeply repressed memories of her failed mourning in relation to Bram and John. The articulation of that mourning, while completely beneficial, occurred in a psychic space where Hagar was out of touch with reality. Now, Hagar is clear-headed and is able to articulate the pain associated with the losses, as well as her involvement with them: "Oh, my two, my dead. Dead by your own hands or by mine? Nothing can take away those years" (292).

The moment is redemptive, however, for Hagar realizes it is not too late to rejoice in the world and to pass on that joy to others. She does so by reaching out to Marvin, and, in doing so, she unequivocally leaves the dark shadows of the past behind. The present, she affirms, is of most importance; and, while she realizes she cannot undo the past, she is in a position to have a positive effect on the present—and that is an opportunity she will not forego any longer.

The first and only opportunity that presents itself to her is with Marvin. In this sequence, Hagar enacts the elemental mother-son relationship that she elided her whole life. She allows him strength over her by admitting her weakness in the face of death: "I can hear my voice saying something, and it astounds me: 'I'm—frightened. Marvin, I'm so frightened—'" (303). Her initial internal response is of the old mode—"What possessed me? I think it's the first time in my life I've ever said such a thing. Shameful"—but then she realizes the positive aspects of her articulation: "Yet somehow it is a relief to speak it" (304). Marvin is now in a position of responsibility over his mother, and the reversal of the parent-child dynamic is not lost on Hagar. By voicing her approval of Marvin, she reinforces his feelings of worth, but she also ensures that her memory will be carried forward in a positive light: "You've been good to me, always. A better son than John" (304). By replacing John with Marvin as her most important parent-child bond, Hagar performs an important action in her work of mourning. She can now feel positive about her own passing, for at least now she has left a memorable legacy. She affirms this conclusion when she articulates her choice of the living over the dead: "The dead don't bear a grudge nor seek a blessing. The dead don't rest uneasy. Only the living" (304).

Hagar Shipley's final moments, as she struggles with the nurse for the glass of water, display the tenacity that marked her temperament her whole life but she is nonetheless changed by her experience of dying. The past is brought back to the present in the work of mourning she undertakes in *The*

Stone Angel, and the beneficial results of that activity allow her to die with some measure of peace.

Laurence ends her first novel in the Manawaka series on a positive note, foreshadowing the four books to come. Her focus on the articulation of grief through the work of mourning in *The Stone Angel* carries over into the remaining texts. Likewise, the pattern of the work of mourning is established in this novel, for each subsequent protagonist finds herself in a liminal state that requires a deeply felt examination of the self that only occurs through active grieving, which Laurence asserts must be accorded by the grieving self before the labour of the work of mourning can occur. Laurence turned her attention to a much younger figure in her next novel, *A Jest of God*. Rachel Cameron, while youthful compared to Hagar, is also in-between life and death when the novel opens, and she too must find the means to articulate the grief that lies hidden—while shadowing her existence—deep in the recesses of her mind.

CHAPTER TWO

TRANSGRESSING THE TABOOS: RACHEL'S WORK OF MOURNING

In her second novel in the Manawaka series, *A Jest of God*, published in 1966, Laurence continues her exploration of the articulation of grief. Like Hagar in *The Stone Angel*, the narrator-protagonist of this novel, Rachel Cameron, struggles not only with deeply entrenched feelings of loss, but she also suffers from the inability to mourn effectively and thus work through those emotions. In contrast with Hagar, however, Rachel recognizes from the outset of the novel that she mourns and that her grief is constricted. Similar to her sister Stacey in the next novel in the series, *The Fire-Dwellers*, Rachel is unable to cope with the loss she feels when the novel opens, and she reels from the conflicting emotions that constriction raises within her. Laurence repeats the pattern in *A Jest of God* that she first set in *The Stone Angel*, and then employs again in

The Fire-Dwellers, whereby mourning is first triggered by emotional experiences the mourner initially does not understand but that facilitate and allow the more controlled, and self-conscious, performance of the work of mourning to occur.

My focus in this chapter is on how Rachel moves out of the static, and thus liminal, state in life she has occupied since her father's death fourteen years previously. In *A Jest of God* Rachel's change is defined as an awakening self that expresses several significant moments of articulation, primarily linked to grief and desire. Several commentators have focussed on articulation. Literary critic Theo Quayle Dombrowski states that "Laurence's characters . . . remain convinced that if they can but explain themselves—that is, make themselves known, not necessarily justify themselves—the terrible spectres of their solitude and confusion will be exorcised," and critic Helen Buss comments that both Rachel and her sister Stacey have a "need to express themselves, and thus to make conscious their true selves." Novelist and critic Aritha van Herk notes that "*A Jest of God* is the noisiest, most wildly eulalic outcry possible. It is the voicing of her discontent, the articulation of her desire."[1]

Mourning has a significant role to play in the movement of Rachel's articulation of her awakening self. At the end of the novel, Rachel has clearly mourned her father and the empty relationship she has with her mother: "I can't know what he was like. He isn't here to say, and even if he were, he wouldn't say, any more than Mother does. Whatever it was that happened with either of them, their mysteries remain theirs. I don't need to know. It isn't necessary. I have my own" (205-206). The work of mourning in *A Jest of God* is a continuum of emotional engagement with grief, beginning subtly and unself-consciously and then progressing to active mourning that ultimately makes an important and fundamental contribution to Rachel's awakening self.

A spectre of death haunts Rachel's existence at the beginning of the novel; Laurence is careful to outline the liminal position in which Rachel finds herself.[2] Laurence emphasizes the role that the death of Rachel's father and her inability to mourn him properly have played in keeping her life stultified; the contrast of this static life with her outbreaks of violent emotion in the first half of the novel is striking and underscores the fact that these outbursts catalyze the self-conscious work of mourning Rachel performs in the second half of the novel.

In "Jesting Within: Voices of Irony and Parody as Expression of Feminisms," literary critic Jill Franks notes, "In the beginning of *A Jest of God*, Rachel is still bound to the original patriarchal figure of her life: her father. She is fascinated by his morbid fascination with death and she has internalized his need for solitude and his melancholy temperament."[3] Similarly, James King points out that "Rachel's sense of profound loss centres on her dead father."[4] Furthermore, in Rachel's world, mourning is a socially codified response fundamentally defined as a denial of death and its effects on the individual, and, thus, her constrainment of the conflicted emotions she feels in relation to her father's death is, in fact, the socially correct, or sanctioned, response. Rachel's thoughts are codified by the denial of death: she fears that "the excuse of grief" (8) is not sufficient to allow for the increasing eccentricity she recognizes in herself. She thinks, "There. I am doing it again. This must stop. Whenever I find myself thinking in a brooding way, I must simply turn it off and think of something else. God forbid that I should turn into an eccentric" (8). Sociologist and death historian Philip Ariès notes in *The Hour of Our Death* that "Society regards mourning as morbid,"[5] and clearly Rachel has incorporated this social stricture into her emotional expression.

In 1955 the social commentator Geoffrey Gorer termed the

growing trend he observed in socially defined responses to death as "the pornography of death": "The natural processes of corruption and decay," he writes, "have become disgusting, as disgusting as the natural processes of birth and copulation were a century ago; preoccupation about such processes is (or was) morbid and unhealthy, to be discouraged in all."[6] Ariès also writes about the elimination from public discourse of matters dealing with death, particularly the emotions attached to issues of death and dying:

> One must avoid—no longer for the sake of the dying person, but for society's sake, for the sake of those close to the dying person—the disturbance and the overly strong and unbearable emotion caused by the ugliness of dying and by the very presence of death in the midst of a happy life, for it is henceforth given that life is always happy or should always seem to be so.[7]

In *The Hour of Our Death*, he extends these comments: "A new situation emerged in the middle part of the twentieth-century. . . . There is a conviction that the public demonstration of mourning, as well as its too-insistent or too-long private expression, is inherently morbid. . . . Mourning is a malady."[8] Ariès and Gorer emphasize that death, its physical realities, and the expression of emotions in response to it, have become taboos in contemporary western societies. Mourning has become an illness or disease to be avoided, rather than a normal function of the life cycle.[9] Rachel, then, has fallen victim to a general societal response to death that removes issues related to death from the public sphere.

Rachel's response to her father's death is compounded by her father's occupation as an undertaker: she is particularly drawn to issues related to death and death practices because of her lack of knowledge of how he led his life. She feels that, to understand him better—and, as a consequence, her relationship with him—she must understand his fascination with the dead. However, her socially conditioned impulse tells her she must retreat from confronting the reality of her father's existence, and this causes a conflict between the need to explore her emotions and the need to submit to social taboos. She cannot bring herself to explore "those rooms on the ground floor" (20) where the mortuary was (and still is), which is where her father "lived away his life" (20). Rachel's need to explore her father's existence, then, also requires her to transgress the social boundaries that define death-related issues as a taboo, and this she has been unable to do. Her fear is that her emotions will take over and subsume her, rather than being beneficial.

So far, then, the work of mourning is completely thwarted for Rachel, and in the early pages of the novel there is no indication that her situation will alter significantly. Before she can find the strength to fulfill her mourning needs, Rachel must be jarred into taking action. To achieve this, Laurence places her protagonist in situations alien to her sensibilities and charged with the emotions of grief and desire. By articulating these emotions Rachel begins her work, albeit unself-consciously, and these scenes, then, lead to her more active engagement in the labour of mourning.

The first two important moments in Rachel's labouring—her outburst in the Tabernacle and her first sexual experience—have similar patterns of emotional engagement for her. Together the two scenes make possible the self-conscious mourning that Rachel actively performs later in the novel, and they must be read in terms of their subtle contributions to her emotional engagement. Both are significant transgressions of the social taboos that have so far bound Rachel's behaviour, thus facilitating her defiance of the conventions that disallow overt mourning later in the book. Throughout her visit to the Tabernacle, Rachel worries that she will be seen by her mother's friends, who would view her attendance there in a

negative light; and, as a single woman, Rachel engages in premarital sex, yet another activity forbidden to her by society's
strictures. In both scenes, Rachel is confronted with a situation completely outside her normal realm of experience, and
the contribution to her work of mourning is primarily because
they are deeply emotional articulations, rather than internalized expressions. Thus, her sense of self is perceptibly shifted,
even if only slightly, so she is no longer quite the same person
that she was previously. It is worth reiterating here that Rachel
has been in a seemingly perpetual state of stasis for fourteen
years: her mourning can only be initiated by powerful forces.

These two moments of articulation are fundamentally
experiences of otherness for Rachel, as the emotional engagement she has occurs completely outside her ordinary realm.
One could say that Rachel is catalyzed (even if unwillingly, as
is the case in the Tabernacle) by words and actions that are
alien to her sensibility, and it is precisely because they are alien
that her emotions are enabled. Russian literary theorist
Mikhail Bakhtin's notion of double-voiced discourse is useful
to understanding how this process functions and how it
becomes significant to her mourning:

> Someone else's words introduced into our own speech
> inevitably assume a new (our own) interpretation and
> become subject to our evaluation of them; that is, they
> become double-voiced.... Our practical everyday speech
> is full of other people's words: with some of them we
> completely merge our own voice, forgetting whose they
> are; others, which we take as authoritative, we use to
> reinforce our own words; still others, finally, we populate
> with our own aspirations, alien or hostile to them.[10]

Literary theorist William McClellan notes that for Bakhtin
"the self, the agent of discourse . . . [is] a fluid subject/site who
constructs herself and her discourse from the already given
utterances of others."[11] In looking at Rachel's experiences, it

will be important to note how the utterances of others work their way into her voicing. At the Tabernacle, for example, Rachel's evening is marked by her difficulties in dealing effectively with a situation alien to her sensibilities, both in terms of the kind of social interaction that forms the core of the evening at the Tabernacle and in the kind of articulation that is celebrated. For Rachel, speaking in tongues is "sinister foolery" (41). The codes of behaviour that have ruled her life dictate that "People should keep themselves to themselves—that's the only decent way" (41). And yet, by appropriating words (even if nonsensical) and actions that would never normally be her own, and seeing in their expression desire and grief, she "populates" them with her own deeply rooted "aspirations," to borrow Bakhtin's terms. That she does not recognize the significance of her articulation is not particularly important: what is significant is that she has finally let loose buried emotion, and the knowledge that she can do so is applied later in the novel to her work of mourning.

The Tabernacle scene is clearly figured as alien to Rachel; the moments leading up to her outburst are described with words and phrases that denote otherness. She feels out of place in the crowded room, thinking of herself as trapped, rather than feeling a part of a congenial community, as Calla does: "I can't move, that's the awful thing. I'm hemmed in, caught" (36). She thinks of the people around her as "other," as indicated by her choice of pronoun: "*They* are all assembled now" (37). She wants "to make myself narrower so I won't brush against anyone" (38). To her, the room is confining and constricting, rather than spiritually awakening. She thinks of it "like some crypt, dead air and staleness, deadness, silence" (37). For the others, there is hope that there will "be ecstatic utterances" (37), which is quite the opposite from the sense of death the scene evokes for Rachel.

Rather than feeling more comfortable as the evening progresses, Rachel becomes more and more disturbed, wishing
that she could leave—"I must leave. I cannot stand this" (40)—
but feeling unable to. When, finally, a man speaks in tongues,
Rachel feels how different from those around her she really is,
for the others are in awe of his outburst, while she feels threat-
ened and is frightened:

> *Galamani halfaka tabinota caragoya lal lal ufranti*—
> Oh my God. They can sit, rapt, wrapped around and
> smothered willingly by these syllables, the chanting of
> some mad enchanter, himself enchanted? It's silly to be
> afraid. But I am. I can't help it. And how can anyone look
> and face anyone else. (41)

In terms of Bakhtin's double-voiced speech, the words
Rachel hears are no more than foolishness, as the spiritual
inspiration of the speaker and his listeners is lost to her.[12] She
only senses the articulation as transgression, as the breaking of
a taboo, for in her own church any sort of articulation is seen
as out of place. On the next Sunday, when she is in church, she
wonders at how an old man can shamelessly sing in church,
despite no longer having a strong voice: "How can he do it?
Doesn't he know how he sounds and how it makes him look?"
(48). She also remembers "a mongoloid boy" who used to
swear in church: "Those Sundays were a torment as pure as
anything I've known since" (48).

The unself-conscious articulation by Rachel that marks the
climax of the scene is perhaps the most alien experience of her
life to date, and it is precisely because it is so out of the ordinary for her that it becomes beneficial to the work of mourning she so very much needs to perform. When she speaks out,
she is at first unaware of her articulation, and it is only after it
is over that she is able to reconstruct and contemplate the significance of her experience:

That voice!
Chattering, crying, ululating, the forbidden transformed cryptically to nonsense, dragged from the crypt,
stolen and shouted, the shuddering of it, the fear, the
breaking, the release, the grieving—
Not Calla's voice. Mine. Oh my God. Mine. The
voice of Rachel. (43)

She appropriates the form of expression of the other speaker
in the congregation in her own articulation, and, thus, her
speech is double-voiced. The original religious or spiritual
intentions are clearly not carried over in her expression, however, and meaning in the sounds she expresses is dependent on
her own personal, and heretofore private, needs and intentions.
Read as double-voiced, Rachel's articulation *becomes* what she
identifies in her words. Within this theorization of discourse,
this can—and indeed must and does—have more than one
meaning. In this passage, too, Laurence reinforces the doubleness of Rachel's language by employing a pun. Her repressed
speech is not only metaphorically kept in the crypt (or buried),
but it is also encrypted and requires decoding.

Rachel interprets her articulation in the first instance as
grief, and this expression of mourning is signalled as a taboo,
as conventional societal behaviour would dictate. The words
are taken from the crypt of her deeply buried grief in what she
at first recognizes as the "release" it actually is. Her adherence
to social codes, however, quickly takes over, and Rachel identifies her speech as deviant rather than as beneficial. She
explains herself to Calla in the most negative of terms: "Do
you know what I detest more than anything else? Hysteria. It's
so slack—. I've never done anything like that before. I'm so
ashamed" (44). Grief is identified, not as a positive articulation, but as unclean or unusual. Philip Ariès remarks in *The
Hour of Our Death* that, in the modern era of responses to
death, "weeping is synonymous with hysteria,"[13] and clearly

Rachel internalizes this interpretation. When Calla tells Rachel she is being too hard on herself, her response is that "I can't be hard enough, evidently. What will I do next, Calla? I'm—oh, Calla, I'm so damn frightened" (44).

In "The Eulalias of Spinsters and Undertakers," Aritha van Herk interprets Rachel's outburst as primarily sexual in nature, seeing it as a sort of "orgasm" that indicates her "eulalic desire . . . [and] her sexual longing."[14] In identifying her expression as hysteria, Rachel acknowledges the sexual desire underlying the impulses that have led to her articulation. However, the connection between *eros* and grief, as with grief and hysteria, is noted in psychoanalytic theory and is applicable to Rachel's situation. In *Loss* John Bowlby remarks that "clinical experience and a reading of the evidence leaves little doubt of the truth of the main proposition [of Freud's "Mourning and Melancholia"]—that much psychiatric illness is an expression of pathological mourning—or that such illness includes many cases of anxiety state, depressive illness and hysteria."[15] The expression of grief is not necessarily subordinated by the movement of desire, but, rather, it is aided by it. The complex mix of emotional impulses Laurence includes in this scene is indicative of her sophisticated understanding of the way that subconsciously rooted emotions affect the most elemental of human actions.

The second experience that prefigures Rachel's self-conscious work of mourning is more overtly sexual, but, as with the Tabernacle scene, she is further prepared for mourning by the significance of emotional engagement and by the shifts in her sense of self. The loss of virginity marks her move into adulthood physiologically, and the new emotions she must learn to deal with, along with the self-confidence she gains, contribute to her ability to transgress the forces that have held her back from grieving for her father's death.

The sex scene represents the next step in Rachel's emotional expression, for she does not actively shy away from emotional engagement. Sex may be new to her, but there is no refusal: *that* dormant part of her psyche will be awakened and will be allowed release. As in the Tabernacle, Rachel is confronted by otherness. Sexual contact with another person is, of course, an alien experience to her, but the sense of otherness is heightened by her partner, Nick Kazlik. He is defined as an other-figure, even though she knew him as a child: Rachel points out that he is of a different cultural background, what is described as the *other* major socio-cultural community in Manawaka: "Half the town is Scots descent and the other half is Ukrainian. Oil, as they say, and water" (71). Her mother disapproves of Nick because he is "the milkman's son" (71). When Rachel is together with him immediately before their union, she contemplates the fact that she is with someone quite alien to her: "I've touched him, touched his face and his mouth. That is all I know of him, his face, the bones of his shoulder. That's not knowing very much" (91).

As the events of the Tabernacle "guided" Rachel into emotional articulation, so does Nick direct her towards sexual fulfillment. He tells her, "You want it, too. You know you do" (96), and then he orders her to "Put it in, darling" (97). Here, as in the Tabernacle, another's speech is recast into her own emotional context, in an example of double-voiced discourse, so that the sexual experience becomes infused with Rachel's conflicted feelings about her father and mother. Nick reassures Rachel that the field he has chosen is "as private as the grave" (96), so no one will see. She populates these words differently, however, thinking first of Andrew Marvell's words in "To His Coy Mistress"—*The grave's a fine and private place / But none, I think, do there embrace* (96)—and then of her parents' dysfunctional marriage: "My mother said, 'One thing about your father, he was never one to make many demands upon me, that's one thing you could say for him'" (96). By thinking of her mother's conservative view of sex, she affirms she is breaking the family taboo against sexual fulfillment.

In a second moment of double-voiced discourse, Rachel acknowledges the breaching of the larger social taboo against premarital sex that is doubly applicable, due to gender biases. Nick tells her "It's never very much good the first time," meaning her lack of an orgasm, and she misinterprets these words to indicate her virginity: "Was it so obvious. . . . That it was the first time, for me?" she asks (98). Misunderstanding her, Nick states: "Don't worry—I don't think you're a tramp" (98). She is still seeing his words only within her own discursive aspirations, however, as she thinks that "I can't see what he means" (98). When she does finally understand him, she sees that the notion of a taboo applying to her situation is quite ridiculous: "[H]e doesn't know how I've wanted to lose that reputation, to divest myself of it as though it were an oxen yoke. . . . I want to laugh" (98). Her laughter is inspired by her recognition that she has allowed a social stricture to repress her sexuality, and this understanding becomes an important moment of learning for her as she realizes the taboo of knowing her father's life and world has haunted her for an equally long time. After she and Nick have had sex, her thoughts affirm that the change is significant for Rachel: "I don't care, I don't care about anything except this peace, this pride, holding him" (98). Desire allowed its articulation, she confirms, erases the strictures that contained her for so long. And so, too, in the next scene she realizes the articulation of the deeply stifled grief for her father's death must be beneficial and necessary.

The link between the lesson learned from expressing desire and the self-conscious work of mourning is immediately evident as Rachel descends to the funeral parlour in the bottom half of the house she shares with her mother, soon after her second experience with Nick. Nora Stovel notes, "Only after she has come to life with Nick does Rachel have the courage to descend to that forbidden nightmare place."[16] She is now finally ready to confront the feelings of grief that have shadowed her life for so long. This descent is literally another breaking of the social taboos that have contained her emotions, like those she has just transgressed in having sex as a single woman, and those earlier in the novel by speaking out in the Tabernacle. This violation of taboo, however, is the most fundamental one, for, as Rachel remembers, "It was in those rooms on the ground floor there, where I was told never to go, that my father lived away his life. All I could think of, then, was the embarrassment of being the daughter of someone with his stock-in-trade" (20).

The secrets of the funeral parlour are both deeply rooted personal and private ones for Rachel, and publicly sanctioned mysteries. This is made evident at the end of the first chapter of the novel, when Rachel has a dream of "descending to the place where I am not allowed" (25), where her father engages in the unspoken, and socially unspeakable, work of embalming and dressing the corpses:

> The silent people are there, lipsticked and rouged, powdered whitely like clowns. How funny they look, each lying dressed in best, and their open eyes are glass eyes, cat's eye marbles, round glass beads, blue and milky, unwinking. (25)

Rachel thinks of her father as a forbidden object, for she cannot reach him: "He is behind the door I cannot open" (25). Even in her dream, her father is dead: "And his voice—his voice—so I know he is lying there among them, lying in state" (25). She thinks of her father as "king of" the corpses (25), but certainly not of his family. Rachel can only allow herself descent to her father's space in a dream at this stage of her mourning, but, after she has experienced two deeply moving emotional experiences, she is ready to go actively where she has heretofore only gone in her imagination.

This scene marks Rachel's first active exploration of her father's world, as well as her first defiance of the strictures that have defined his space as forbidden. Her encounter with Hector, the undertaker who took over her father's business, is particularly important, for he guides her through the business and the commodified nature of funerary practice. Unlike her father, he is the undertaker who explains himself, and so Hector becomes a sort of surrogate father-figure. Additionally, Hector is like Nick in that he is essentially different from Rachel, and he draws emotional articulation out of Rachel, as the otherness of the Tabernacle and the sexual experience brought emotion to the fore. In this scene, however, Rachel is self-conscious about the implications of her grief, and she is aided by its expression.

When she descends the stairs, Rachel is still bound by the familial strictures, for she fears that her mother will hear her: "The carpet makes the stairs silent, but not silent enough. If she wakens, I'll say I forgot to lock the downstairs door" (124). This moment of transgression is contrasted by Rachel's ascent at the end of the scene; now she no longer fears her mother's possible reprimands, taking on the voice of authority instead: "If she wakens, all I have to say is hush. Hush, now, sh, it's all right, go to sleep now, never fear, it's nothing" (134). In-between these moments, Rachel has forced herself to cross the bounds of her socially and familially dictated behaviour, and has thus consciously engaged in the work of mourning.

The door to the funeral chapel invokes an imaginative or dream-like atmosphere to Rachel's approach, inviting her back into her interior world of the mind, rather than into the concrete engagement with the "matter" of her father's life. The door is "shinily varnished . . . fitted with wrought-iron staves and loops and swirls, so it looks like the door of a keep or a castle prison, but false, a mock-up" (124). Rachel's thoughts connote masquerade and artifice: she terms the parlour "Ye Olde Dungeon," not real at all but like "a Disney film, where even the children know that the inmates are cartoons" (124). The sense of a Disney film is interesting, for the image represents artifice at its highest level: the world of fantasy. And yet, by attempting to continue on with her exploration, Rachel is entering a world where the physical task of preparing bodies for burial is performed—far removed from the world of fantasy.

The thoughts running through Rachel's mind as she approaches the door of the funeral home reinforce the impression of transgression. Rachel hesitates ("I hesitate to knock" [125]) and questions her actions, the voice of her father echoing in her thoughts: "What am I doing here? I should be asleep. This is no place for you, Rachel. Run along now, there's a good girl. This is no place for you" (124). That she continues on, in defiance of her father's voice, is the strongest indication that Rachel is ready to confront her emotional constrainment so that she can now, finally, work through the emotions linked with her father's death.[17]

When Hector answers the knocking on the door, Rachel again gives the impression she is interested in taking charge of her own emotional unease, for she is active in asking for admittance to the funeral home, first thinking the words and then speaking them: "Let me come in" (125). By asking to be let in, Rachel commands the situation, rather than allowing it to control her, as happens so frequently. Hector asks Rachel into the workroom, the inner domain of Niall's practice, and she feels like she is continuing to break down the walls that distanced herself from her father. She thinks, "I couldn't have been in here more than a couple of times in my life. He always said, when I hovered, 'This is no place for you'" (126).

Rachel is welcomed into the chapel by Hector and enters

into the private room where the embalming and preparation of the body takes place. The next scenes are a mixture of the search for signs of her father and educational moments when Rachel learns more about how her society codifies and sanctions death.

Hector details his philosophy and his approach to the job of dealing with the dead as well as with the mourners. His choice of words reflects the commodified nature of his business, laying bare the aspects of his occupation that society denies, and therefore he breaks the social stricture that denies the realities of death. Thus, his candid conversation with Rachel helps her to understand more fully the roots of her constricted mourning: "It's all a question of presentation, that's what I say. Presentation is All. Everybody knows a product has to be attractively packaged—it's the first rule of sales, isn't that so? Well, this is a little tricky in my line of trade, as you can well appreciate" (127).

Hector defines his role in the funeral process as a kind of manager-figure who controls and takes charge of dealing with death for the mourners. Hector is speaking specifically of the time immediately after a death has occurred, and, while the commodified nature of his business plan is tacitly critiqued by Laurence, he is able to provide some grief management for Rachel. She has needed to find some kind of effective structure to her mourning for so many years, and Hector's methods become useful and necessary to her work of mourning. Hector tells her that he "sell[s] two things. . . . One: *Relief.* Two: *Modified Prestige*" (127). Hector's ideas are based on the fact that people are very uncomfortable with the physicality of death and wish to distance themselves from that. Coming even before grief, remorse, and sorrow, is, in Hector's words, "panic—what'll we do with the body?" (127). And this is where the manager comes into play: "The prime purpose of a funeral director is not all this beautician deal which some

members of the profession go in for so much. No. It's this—
to take over" (127). The management of grief has become a
consumable commodity, packaged, impersonalized, evading
the very real emotional needs of mourners, but for Rachel, the
commodity Hector has to offer is knowledge of her father and
his way of life, and, in his "management" of her grief, he
guides her expertly through the conflicts that have haunted
her.

Now that she finally is in the forbidden space, Rachel realizes there is, in fact, nothing of her father here: "my eyes are
searching the room, and yet this is senseless. Nothing is as it
used to be, and there's nothing left from then, nothing of him,
not a clue" (129). She is, however, still engaged emotionally by
the experience of being in the funeral home, as she realizes she
is speaking with emotion: "My voice has gone high and atten-
uated with some hurt I didn't know was there" (130). This
emotion, she quickly understands, is ripe to be explored—to
be confronted as the work of mourning would require. The
room, from Rachel's perspective, now becomes a place where
grief can be engaged, or performed: "the room looks all at
once different, a room set nowhere, the stage-set of a drama
that never was enacted" (130). With the aid of Hector, Rachel
more fully explores her understanding of her father. She
thinks of Hector as a "comic prophet, dwarf seer" (131), for he
dispels the myth Rachel has built up of Niall as a victim of
life's circumstances. As Hector says, "I would bet he had the
life he wanted most" (131). And, as she contemplates in
response, "*The life he wanted most*. If my father had wanted
otherwise, it would have been otherwise. Not necessarily better, but at least different" (131).

Freed from this myth of Niall's existence, Rachel comes to
the realization that, if her father had the choice to change his
life, despite circumstances that seemed to work against him,
then she, too, has that ability: "Did he ever try to alter it? Did

I, with mine?" (131). Thus, by a new envisioning of her father's life, Rachel is herself beginning to be freed from victimhood.

In the next sequence of her visit to the funeral home, Rachel is taken on a tour of the chapel, which functions as a ritual funeral service directed by Hector. Once inside the chapel, despite its highly artificial decor,[18] Rachel is indeed mourning: "I collapse on to the hard mourners' bench where the family is meant to sit" (132). Allowing emotion to overcome her, as Hector plays a hymn, Rachel comes to another moment of awareness about herself and about her father and her grief: "there is nothing here for me except what is here now—" (133). In transgressing the social taboos to confront the shadow of her father, she realizes that the shadow was, in the end, mostly of her own making: there is, after all, no mystery lurking in the funeral home that, if unearthed, will consume her.[19]

Stepping out of the shadow of her father's constrainment on her life also forces Rachel to be more self-reliant, as Stovel notes: "Rachel realizes that she cannot control her father's (or mother's) life or death, but she *can* control her own."[20] Indicative of Rachel's new-found ability to accept her father as he was are her imaginings of him had he continued living, before and after the descent to see Hector. Rachel's visions of her father are constructed primarily out of his absence, for, even in life, he was scarcely an active member of the family, preferring, instead, to hide away in the mortuary. And thus, after his death, Rachel can only relate to her father through this absence of knowledge. In one episode early in the novel, Rachel walks through Manawaka and imagines what would have become of her father had he not died prematurely:

> On the steps of the Queen Victoria Hotel a few old men sit, absorbing the sunlight through their grey buttoned-up sweaters and loose grey unpressed trousers,

talking in thin voices. Perhaps if my father were alive, he'd be there with them. He'd be about that age by now, I guess. I hate to think of him like that, crinkled face not properly shaven, an Adam's apple moving up and down in a scrawny throat. (67)

Here, Rachel is embarrassed by thoughts of her father as a socially marginalized figure. Later, after she has descended to the funeral home, she has a renewed vision of his place in her life and in society. In this episode, Rachel returns to the Queen Victoria Hotel, but, rather than feeling shame at the decrepit old men she sees, she feels remorse for her previous thoughts: "If I went in there now, unbidden, young to them, strange in my white raincoat, and said *Forgive me*, they would think I had lost my mind" (169). She is, of course, asking for forgiveness from her father for having denounced him.

She can now no longer use the excuse of grief for her father as a reason for her victimhood. Rachel must learn to stop mourning her own suspended life so she can move on and grow into a fully individuated person. Rachel has now worked through many of the conflicts in relation to her father that haunted her life since his death, but she has not yet completed her work of mourning. The sense of self that was shattered by his death, what Anthony Giddens terms the "shattered sense of ontology," still needs to be reconstructed. This is made evident when Rachel feels trapped by her fears of pregnancy. She seeks solutions external to herself by appealing to Calla, and then imagining Nick and her sister somehow aiding her, only to realize she is completely alone and must be courageously self-reliant. The pathway to this self-reliance, however, is a difficult one and almost costs her life, as she considers suicide. In surviving, she has learned to find the strength within herself to alter her life. She discovers that, to have a better life, she must take action on her own behalf.

There are two moments prior to the suicide attempt where

Rachel contemplates reaching out to others. She considers
writing to Nick for help, but immediately understands that
this is not a viable option: "No. He can't. No one. There isn't
anyone. I'm on my own. I never knew before what that would
be like. It means no one. Just that. Just—just myself" (171).
And then, a few pages later, when she thinks of reaching out
to her sister, she realizes her sister cannot provide answers,
either: "if I could talk to you, you would maybe be the only
person I could talk to. Look—would you know? ... God damn
her. What could she possibly know?" (174).

Finding that she cannot reach out for answers, and finding
also that there are no inner ones, Rachel decides to kill herself.
Her final thoughts before moving to suicide demonstrate the
dilemma she feels she is in: "It can't be borne. I can't see any
way it could be. It can't be ended, either. I don't know where
to go" (175). Ironically, her means encompass both her mother's addiction to sleeping pills and her father's alcoholism, as
she plans to use both. While she is swallowing pills and drinking the whiskey, Rachel's thoughts focus on the beneficial
nature of her actions: "Come on, Rachel. Only a little way to
go, and then everything will be all right" (176). In a disruption
similar to the two previous moments when she has involun-
tarily acted—in the Tabernacle with Calla and when she struck
her student James Doherty—Rachel unconsciously resists the
will to die by throwing the remaining pills out the window,
rather than swallowing them. This moment of disruption
causes not confusion, as in the previous cases, but clarity of
mind: she discovers that dying is not the answer to her problems and there must be another way:

> At that moment, when I stopped, my mind wasn't
> empty or paralyzed. I had one clear and simple thought.
> *They will all go on in somehow, all of them, but I will be*
> *dead as stone and it will be too late then to change my mind.*
> (176)

Although nothing has actually changed, Rachel has gained a new understanding of her situation: "Only one thing has changed—I'm left with it, with circumstances, whatever they may be. I can't cope and I can't opt out" (177). She now reaches out, albeit with little belief, to God as the Other voice in her mind. More importantly, however, comes the recognition that her inability to solve her problems has been the inhibiting factor in her life. She asks herself, recognizing and acknowledging loss, "How many sores did I refuse to let heal?" (177), thereby beginning the steps toward repairing the self shattered by loss.

This new, if not fully understood, confidence in acting for herself is manifested in the final sequences of *A Jest of God* when Rachel makes the decision to see Dr. Raven about her suspected pregnancy. Rather than responding to the voice in her head that tells her she "can't go to the doctor's" (178), she forcefully tells herself, "You've got to do something" (179). This assertive manner is a strong response to the taboos that forbid single motherhood. Dr. Raven tells her he suspects a tumour, and suddenly Rachel feels grief again: "and then only that other voice, wordless and terrible, the voice of some woman mourning her lost children" (187). She mourns the loss of the child she wanted after all, but what needs to be signalled here is that she mourns her own loss, rather than allowing the loss to control and affect her, as her father's death did. That she goes to Winnipeg by herself for the operation affirms the command she now has of her life, and that she returns from the city even stronger and more self-assured than before marks the end of the work of mourning. The choices she now makes, to move to Vancouver against her mother's wishes, are in her own best interest and serve her emotional needs.

At the end of the novel she comes to an understanding of the role of narratives of ancestry in her life. She revisits the funeral home downstairs, and realizes that the ghosts that may remain there are best left to lie, and, indeed, that the ghosts have now been put to rest. The dominating narrative in her life is now her own:

> The last time I was in the Japonica Funeral Chapel was that night I came down here late and talked to Hector. Everything looked just the same, but now it does not seem to matter much that my father's presence has been gone from here for a long time. I can't know what he was like. He isn't here to say, and even if he were, he wouldn't say, any more than Mother does. Whatever it was that happened with either of them, their mysteries remain theirs. I don't need to know. It isn't necessary. I have my own. (206)

Like the narrator in the poem "Losers" by Carl Sandburg, that Laurence uses as the epigraph to the novel, Rachel must pass a tomb and reflect:

> *If I should pass the tomb of Jonah*
> *I would stop there and sit for awhile;*
> *Because I was swallowed one time deep in the dark*
> *And came out alive after all.*

In Rachel's case, it is her father's tomb where she must spend time contemplating the effect he has had on her life, but Rachel must also acknowledge that she needs to stop and reflect upon the malaise that afflicts her. Only then can her life go on.

Laurence ends *A Jest of God* on an ambiguously positive note. Rachel has clearly moved beyond the constriction that plagued her for so many years, but at the same time she is unsure of what the future holds for her: "Where I'm going, anything may happen. Nothing may happen" (208). What is important is that, through her work of mourning—through the confrontation with the losses she suffers from—she is able to face uncertainty and to ultimately escape the spectre of death.

In the next novel she was to write, *The Fire-Dwellers*, Laurence presents another character who has difficulty finding and articulating her voice amid a constricting world. Stacey MacAindra is Rachel's sister, of course, and, thus, the parallels and differences between the two experiences of mourning become quite interesting. For both, the work of mourning is carried out *in spite of* social forces that constrict it, and for both the work is carried out in a highly private manner. Laurence is interested in depicting the failure of western societies in dealing with the needs of mourners, and the sister novels become important statements about how individuals fashion their own works of mourning.

CHAPTER THREE

THE CRISIS OF WORD AND MEANING: THE WORK OF MOURNING AND THE LOSS OF CONSOLATION

In *The Fire-Dwellers*, the third novel set in Canada, Laurence continues her exploration of the mourner's shift from the internalization of her grief to its articulation. Like Hagar in *The Stone Angel* and Rachel in *A Jest of God*, Stacey, the narrator-protagonist, finds herself in a liminal state where she is unable to cope with the world around her and where she can see no viable way out of her predicament. Similar to the earlier protagonists, the move through liminality takes the form of a work of mourning. Like her sister Rachel in *A Jest of God*, Stacey is aware that the emotions she feels are linked to loss and that she struggles with social and cultural codes of responding to loss that fail to legitimize her grief.

When *The Fire-Dwellers* opens, Stacey is in a state of crisis where she must either learn to cope with her urban world and domestic life or abandon it completely. Laurence defines Stacey's predicament as a failure of consolation, and it becomes her statement on the harsh reality of late-twentieth-century urban life.[1] How does one, she asks, perform the work of mourning while knowing full well it will never end? Should one "cope" through withdrawal, as Stacey does initially by resorting to alcohol? Or should one turn to another form of escape by leaving urban life behind to begin anew in the countryside, as Stacey also contemplates in her utopian fantasies?

The loss Stacey feels is akin to the losses the other protagonists suffer in the Manawaka fiction. Her losses encompass a range of feelings, including a lack of fulfillment in her life. However, her loss is greater than a mere lack of satisfaction with life, for she feels a shattering of ontological security: her life does not *mean* in any unified or whole way. Sigmund Freud defines grief as the loss of a person or an ideal, and this latter notion applies centrally to Stacey's situation.[2] The novel demonstrates her feelings of loss in relation to her vision of an ideal past and present. Furthermore, since her grief is not legitimized by her society, thus denying her adequate coping structures and strategies, her loss is intensified.

Stacey's work of mourning is figured as three distinct movements carried out over the course of *The Fire-Dwellers*. The first involves Stacey's failed attempts at mourning her world: in the early chapters of the novel, she spends much of her time contemplating the state of her life, without seeing a viable way out of her predicament. The second movement comprises stark departures from her everyday, mundane existence: she takes a ride with her husband's friend Buckle in his truck, attempts to have sex with him in his mother's dilapidated apartment, and she drives into the countryside outside Vancouver and takes a lover many years her junior. These experiences are marked by their elemental otherness to her normal existence, and they jar her out of her stultifying and unsatisfactory life. The final movement in the work of mourning is reflective and evaluative: Stacey realigns her view of her life by legitimizing her grief—thus mourning effectively, in spite of the state of the contemporary world—and by articulating it to her husband.

At the beginning of *The Fire-Dwellers*, Stacey is unable to come to grips with her world, seeing no way out of her predicament: she feels herself to be in a seemingly constant state of grief, and her attempts at working through this feeling are ineffective. Stacey's life is marked by reaction to the world that surrounds her, rather than by active engagement with it, as Stovel notes: "Stacey's operative word is 'cope'—something that she finds it harder and harder to do."[3] This depiction is concomitant with what philosopher George Steiner has called the "failure of consolation" and the "crises of word and meaning" that "have disrupted traditional Western apprehensions of the possibilities of transcendental significance in experience."[4]

The early sections of *The Fire-Dwellers*, then, chart the failure of religiously defined, ritualized, or externally ordered mourning for Stacey and define her attempts at performing the work of mourning effectively. Stacey faces the crisis of the validity of her own voice and the legitimacy of her emotional responses to the world around her, thinking of these feelings as "pre-mourning" and determining them as a condition of life in her era. When she tells the instructor of her Aspects of Contemporary Thought class that she had "worried for twenty years and couldn't seem to stop" (15), she is told that "pre-mourning is a form of self-indulgence" (15). Stacey mistakenly views her instructor as a voice of institutionalized authority and gives her the power to legitimize her emotional expression. With these judgements, Stacey begins to feel that her unease with the world is unreasonable and that one should not lament the state of the world. It is "[l]unatic," as Mac tells her, to do so. Nonetheless, Stacey questions these assumptions about the validity of mourning the world: "Why should I think it unbalanced to want to mourn? Why shouldn't I wail like the widows of Ashur if I feel like it? I have cause" (38). As soon as she has made this pronouncement, however, she resists: "Come, come, Stacey, act your age. That's precisely what I am doing, God, if you really want to know. Too much mental baggage. ... Things keep spilling out of the suitcases, taking me by surprise, bewildering me as I stand on the plat-form" (38). The word "bewildering" is perhaps most telling here, as Stacey feels trapped by her very existence. She does not trust her emotions, as her social world does not legitimize their expression. Thus, she abdicates authority over her self and her deep feelings of loss at the world.

As in *A Jest of God*, Laurence underscores the necessity of mid-twentieth-century mourning practices that are not hindered by the denial of death in western societies.[5] Writing about elegy, literary critic Jahan Ramazani notes the responses of twentieth-century elegists to the changed social reality they encounter:

> Modern elegies betray in their difficult, melancholic mourning the impossibility of preserving a pristine space apart, of grieving for the dead amid the speed and pressure of modern life. Unlike elegies of nostalgic "comfort," the embittered elegies of Hardy, Stevens, Owen, Plath, and others both react against and incorporate the suppression of mourning.[6]

Like the elegists writing before her, Laurence is unable to escape the suppression of grief in the twentieth century and most notably confronts in these two novels the difficulties of performing the work of mourning in a society that does not authorize it.[7] And, like the elegists, her strategy of dealing with these difficulties is through acknowledgement and by having Rachel and Stacey fashion their own ways for carrying out the labour of mourning, despite the impediments they encounter.[8]

Mourning, in the early parts of *The Fire-Dwellers*, is thwarted by Stacey's abdication of authority over herself and by her feelings of loss, as she is unable to find any legitimacy in her own voice. Her sense of bewilderment at the multiple discourses that strike at her is exemplified by her thoughts as she attempts to cope with the world outside her:

> *Everything drifts. Everything is slowly swirling, philosophies tangled with the grocery lists, unreal-real anxieties like rose thorns waiting to tear the uncertain flesh, nonentities of thoughts floating like plankton, green and orange particles, seaweed—lots of that, dark purple and waving, sharks with fins like cutlasses, herself held underwater by her hair, snared around auburn anchor chains.* (34)

These thoughts are set amid the polarities that define Stacey's life: her identity has been lost in the chaos of modern living, even though her life is, on the surface, an ideal one, for she lives the stereotypical suburban life, with a husband, four children, and a nice house. She oscillates between the polarities of the seemingly ideal suburban life and the disorder of contemporary life, never sure where she should situate herself: "What's left of me? Where have I gone? . . . How to get out? This is madness. I'm not trapped. I've got everything I always wanted" (70). Beneath the surface of the suburban utopian fantasy, of course, lies a much harsher reality where meaning is unsure and slippery: "I'm surrounded by voices all the time but none of them seem to be saying anything, including mine" (77).

Voices emanating from television and popular magazines chatter at Stacey, overwhelming her attempts at coming to terms with the grief she feels and that is ironically triggered by those very voices: "Everything is happening on TV. . . . I

probably exaggerate. Do I? *Doom everywhere* is the message I
get. A person ought not to be affected, maybe" (57-58). She
feels powerless in response to the stories of war that the TV
news brings into her life: "I can't listen. It's too much too
much too much. What can you do, anyhow? Nothing. Just
agonize. Useless. All useless. Me included" (89). The headline
Stacey responds to is: "EIGHT-THIRTY NEWS BOMBERS LAST
NIGHT CLAIMED A DECISIVE VICTORY FOUR VILLAGES TOTALLY
DESTROYED AND A NUMBER OF OTHERS SET ABLAZE" (89).
Magazines offer equally impenetrable modern realities for
her, such as the series of headlines she encounters:

> 'Salad Days—Here's How to be Slim in the Swim.'
> Stacey looks frowningly at the mound of edible vegeta-
> tion in the colour photograph, and quickly flicks the
> page. 'Icings with Spicings.' Flick. 'A Nervous
> Breakdown Taught Me Life's Meaning.' Flick. (153)

Here is another example of the effect of magazine articles on
Stacey: "'Nine Ways the Modern Mum May Be Ruining Her
Daughter.' I should never read them, but I always do, and then
I check in my mind to see how many ways I'm ruining Katie.
But how can I tell?"(17). The randomness of her page-turning
underscores the lack of meaning inherent in the magazine
articles. The "flicking" is indicative of her hope that the pages
will somehow randomly open to something that will bring
legitimacy to her existence and perhaps help her mourn
effectively.

Further polarities define Stacey's life as her grief is figured
as encompassing paradoxical oppositions of loss. She idealizes
the past and mourns its loss, and she envisions the present as
a hellish, apocalyptic world where traditional forms of consolation offer no reprieve. Mourning for a happy past is
expressed through memories of a time early in her married life
when ideals seemed possible and marriage was a positive state

of being. Now her deteriorating marriage is defined as a constant struggle of individual identity against patriarchal structures of oppression. Stacey also feels loss through her perception that the world outside her offers no possibility for consolation. She sees the city she lives in, Vancouver, as a cold and hard place where people are subsumed by the chaos of urban life. In one description, Stacey views the buildings in downtown Vancouver as "charred, open to the impersonal winds, glass and steel broken like vulnerable live bones, shadows of people frog-splayed on the stone like in that other city" (14-15).[9] The negative cityscape represents the loss of ideal surroundings and is opposed by a utopian countryside that exists largely in Stacey's imaginative ruminations. The ideal of meaningful spiritual structures is negated in Stacey's rejection of the traditional manifestations of God and religion and of alternate forms of healthy spiritual living, as evident in her scepticism concerning the Richalife formula with which Mac appears to be so enamoured. Stacey is insecure about her belief in a Christian God, but also in her fear that, even if God existed, he would make no difference. In effect, she mourns her own loss of faith in the face of the troubles of the world, longing for an existence where social and spiritual codes of behaviour provide authoritative and satisfying structures for dealing with loss.[10]

Stacey's feelings of loss are aligned along two distinct patterns: urban and rural life. Existence in the city is related to a symbolism of negativity, and it is in urban life that she feels imprisoned. Cityscapes are seen as individual-consuming, and family life and marriage as restricting. Rural life, on the other hand, is equated with happiness in the past and with escape in the future. Stacey's happy memories of marriage all relate to interaction with nature and life away from the city, and it is to a rural space that Stacey escapes, in search of consolation, when she can no longer cope with her life with Mac and the family.[11]

As with *The Stone Angel* and *A Jest of God*, Laurence alludes to elements of pastoral elegy in these passages of the novel. The revisiting of the ideal past is a central feature of conventional elegies, such as "Lycidas" where the elegist looks back to the happy past when he and Lycidas frolicked happily in the fields, and Matthew Arnold's "Thyrsis" where the elegist recalls the happy past when he and Thyrsis walked in the woods and fields in search of intellectual enlightenment. Like Shelley's "Adonais" and "Thyrsis,"[12] the world outside the pastoral landscape is figured as a place of strife and conflict.[13]

Stacey searches for meaning in the world around her, but only finds further loss. The damaging effects of urban space are delineated when Stacey goes into downtown Vancouver and encounters the city—a place alien to her sensibilities. The trip is initiated by her need to get away from her domestic duties, but she is bombarded with sights and sounds that seem to come from all directions. In this space, traditional forms of meaning no longer have certainty. Stacey wonders at the inscription on the war memorial she passes: *"Their Names Shall Live Forevermore . . . Does It Mean Nothing to You.* No question mark" (10). Competing with this vision of unquestioning conviction are other, less convincing, inscriptions she encounters in the window of the nearby Ben's Economy Mart: *"Get a Load of This Bargain Only $10.95, How About This at $4.75? We're Cheating Ourselves at $9.95"* (10). This juxtaposition of discourses causes her feeling that hierarchies of meaning have been lost: different levels of everyday discourse have parity, rather than one having authority over another. Where the certainty of the soldiers' names remain inscribed for eternity (or, at least, for as long as the cenotaph remains), the "sale" signs that intrude on Stacey's awareness contain an urgency that indicates the fleetingness of their inscription. And yet, despite this fleetingness, the signs manage to displace the legitimacy of war losses that the memorial is intended to signal, and thus they underscore the realigned hierarchies of value in the predominantly consumer culture in which Stacey lives. What she realizes in this scene is that the cenotaph no longer has the memorial function implied by permanence as a structure; rather, the intrusion of the sale signs into her consciousness underscores the loss of definite meaning in the contemporary: things that use to mean in uncomplicated ways no longer do so.

By contrast, the world beyond the city is more definitely determined by Stacey as a world of freedom and possibility, and, above all, as a world of escape from the noise and bustle of city and family life. She feels that to get away from her world will be a viable way of coping, and, thus, mourning. Early in the novel she imagines the distant mountains she sees from her house as a place of escape:

> Sometimes I look through the living-room window at the snow mountains, far off, and I wish I could go there, just for a while, with no one else around and hardly any sounds at all, the winds muttering, maybe, and the snow in weird sculptures and caverns, quiet. (15)

Later, when she thinks about Mac's job as a travelling salesman, she considers his travelling in romanticized terms. Nature is benevolent, supplying comfort and insulation from the world of cities: "I'd like to be on the road. Not for anything but just to be going somewhere"—to be away from here:

> *Mac on the road, soaring along as though the old Chev were a winged chariot, through the mountains and the turquoise air, into the valley where the rivers run with names like silkenly flowing water, Similkameen, Tulameen, Coquihalla, the names on maps, clear brown water over the shifting green stones, where the pine and tamarack and the thin spruce trees stand a little way off, blue-green needles dry in the dry gold air, where the tall barbed grasses are never touched or cut but remain eternally high with their pale seedheads like oats bent*

in the light wind that blows always, where it is sun all the way
in the fields of purple fireweed where only the bees make their
furred music. (22)

The places are "names on maps," rather than real places she has ever visited, and thus are only the products of her thoughts. Nature, in this imaginative construction, is benevolent and untouched by civilization.

When she contemplates escape from the worries of her city life, Stacey imagines she would then have the mental space to solve her problems: "I would sort out and understand my life, that is what I would do, if you really want to know" (159). Effective mourning would be possible in a world like this. She imagines the happy summer days she spent with her parents and sister at Diamond Lake, and then she imagines a future scene "somewhere in the Cariboo" where she is a school-teacher. The scene is idyllic, and family life is easily managed in "an old converted barn" (160). Linked with this imagining is a memory of her eighteen-year-old self swimming in Diamond Lake:

> She was a strong swimmer, and when she reached the place where she could see the one spruce veering out of the rock on the distant point, she always turned back, not really accepting her limits, believing she could have gone across the lake.... Stacey, swimming back to shore, coming up for air intermittently, knowing with no doubt that she would make it fine. (161)

Here Stacey is strong and full of certainty, symbolically protected by the water of the lake, rather than being subsumed by it. Water in this scene also opposes fire to reinforce the novel's title and the theme of Stacey's world being on fire. After this memory, Stacey makes an important link between her utopian imaginings of a perfect life in the north and her idyllic memories of Diamond Lake:

Okay. I see it, Sir. I didn't see it before, but I see it now. Thanks for nothing. That's the place I want to get away to, eh? The Cariboo? Up north? No. I've never been any of those places. . . . When I imagine it, it always looks like Diamond Lake. Like, I guess I mean, everything will be just fine when I'm eighteen again. (161)

The past, then, is figured as a lost ideal: pre-marriage, pre-children, pre-responsibility, and pre-city life. That she not only yearns for her more innocent past, but that she, in fact, openly mourns its passing, is clear and is reinforced by her memories of the early days of her marriage: "I got married sixteen years ago and I thought he was like Agamemnon King of Men . . . only that view couldn't last all that long how could it if you are with somebody all the time and see how they go to sleep with their mouth open" (181). Several other passages reinforce these impressions of the past. In one memory sequence Stacey notes a younger and happier self:

Once I was different.
Stacey, travelling light, unfearful in the sun, swimming outward as though the sea were shallow and known, drinking without indignity, making spendthrift love in the days when flesh and love were indestructible. (71)

Spiritually, too, Stacey finds little solace in her view of the tumultuous world. When she thinks of Mac's father, who is a minister, she considers her lack of firm religious belief: "I long to tell him I don't see life his way—gentle Jesus meek and mild and God's in heaven all's right with the world. . . . God knows why I chat to you, God—it's not that I believe in you. Or I do and I don't. Like echoes in my head" (63). Her lack of belief, however, is distinctly figured as a loss. She laments the departure of such certainty in her life: "I want to tell [the children]. What? That I mourn my disbelief? I don't tell them, though. I go along with the game" (68). Religion and God are a game, rather than a shaping and life-affirming belief system: God as a concept fails to provide consolation for the world's troubles. Stacey refers to faith in a different context when she is on the peace march that she quickly abandons for lack of conviction: "[A]ll I can feel is embarrassment. I might at least have the decency not to feel embarrassed. Maybe I'd feel different if I had faith. But I can't seem to manage it" (251).

The shift away from feeling grief in the face of her world occurs when Stacey feels unable to continue with her life as it is. She finds herself in a liminal state where she desires a past she cannot return to, while she finds the present situation to be untenable: "I am not sure that I want to continue on living at all. I can't cope" (130). She fears she will become one of the living dead by drinking herself into a stupor, as her father did: "It's the ones who say good-bye before they're dead who bug me" (129). She wonders if her life will continue its down slide: "Sometimes a person feels that something else must have been meant to happen in your own life, or is this all there's ever going to be, just like this? Until I die" (120). This sense of a meaningless void in life, what could be described as a sort of existential liminality, brings Stacey, like her sister Rachel, to the point of contemplating suicide. Nora Stovel notes that "the handgun that [Stacey] has hidden in her own basement . . . [is] a potent symbol of death or suicide, the great escape," and critic Allan Bevan remarks that "In this novel . . . death is never far away."[14] Thus, Stacey always feels that the option of taking her life is within reach.

The catalyst for the work of mourning is the occasion when Stacey, quite drunk, accidentally burns herself on the kitchen stove:[15] "She reaches for the frying pan, stumbles, puts out a hand to balance herself. The hand lands on the edge of the electrical scarlet circle" (130). While not volitional, Stacey reads the situation as such, noting that she needs to explain the action, although it is an accident: "How to explain this?

Anybody can explain anything if they put their mind to it"
(130). Stacey's awareness of the burn is indicative of the mental state she is in, for the language used denotes an automatic
response. She feels the pain without knowing what it is: "It
hurts it hurts it hurts what is it" (130). The break after the
expression of pain before the questioning indicates discon-
nectedness from the action (and from her physical self), as
does the lack of the question mark itself. The lack of punctu-
ation indicates the lack of emotion of her response. This automatic mode is carried over into Stacey's next action: "She has
without knowing it pulled her hand away. She regards it with
curiosity" (130). Like the initial burning, Stacey's actions stem
from somewhere deeper than the conscious mind. It is as if,
through the burn, the physical pain is attempting to penetrate
her mind already numbed by the subsuming discourses of her
life and, now, by alcohol as well. Stacey identifies the burn
marks on her hand as "My brand of stigmata" (130). Feeling
her life not lived effectively and feeling disgraced, Stacey sees
few options for her continued existence.

Unsure about how to reach out to change her life, Stacey
appeals to her husband in a mental dialogue:

> Mac—I'm scared. Help me. But it goes a long way back.
> Where to begin? What can I possibly say to you that you
> will take seriously? What would it need, with you, what
> possible cataclysm, for you to say anything of yourself to
> me? What should I do? (130)

Stacey's sense that the appeal to Mac would only end in failure
leads her to question her very existence: "I'm not sure I really
want to go on living at all" (130).

This scene, while brief, is paradigmatic of her mourning,
for Stacey is primarily impelled by a volition unknown to her.
The scene also marks the first instance in her work of mourning where she actively explores the areas of emptiness in her

life. Her encounters with Buckle and Luke are attempts at filling the void of intimacy with her husband. With Luke, Stacey returns psychically and physically to her youth and the utopian possibilities of the rural world. Evident in these experiences is Stacey's desire to perform the recuperative labour of mourning by replacing what she has lost with new associations. There is no conscious attempt at the reparation of loss here. The second movement of her grief work begins when Stacey makes a commitment to reparation and acceptance of loss, and, ultimately, to herself.

Stacey's first big step outside her domesticated life is when she goes for a ride with Buckle. The drive with Buckle is her attempt to recover the lost elements of her marriage, such as intimacy and the ability to communicate effectively. In this sequence Stacey imagines a new and dangerous, but also exhilarating, life for herself. Buckle lives on the edge when he drives his truck; Stacey is enthralled by that energy, and she enjoys being perceived as a dangerous woman by being associated with him.

Buckle urges Stacey to take a quick trip with him to Coquitlam on one of his deliveries, but Stacey is impelled by something beyond the purely conscious, for she notes: "Then, without thinking or knowing she is going to do it, she climbs into the truck beside Buckle" (140). The ride with Buckle is figured as a betrayal of Mac, as Stacey thinks when she reveals her dissatisfaction with Mac's long hours: "Traitor. How can you speak about Mac to anyone else? It's no one else's business" (141). Stacey imagines her world falling apart, reinforcing the central thematics of the novel: "*The house is burning. Everything and everyone in it. Nothing can put out the flames. The house wasn't fire-resistant. One match was all it took*" (141). The domestic sphere obliterated, Stacey imagines Buckle and herself out on "*The northern highway, uncrowded*," in a sexual scenario: "*He is poised above her—hard, ready, taut—and she can hardly wait for him"* (141). Buckle tells her a story about his games of "chicken" on the highway, and, along with the sexual fantasy, Stacey is enraptured by the perilous nature of her association with him. When they arrive at the warehouse, Stacey is "delighted" that she is perceived by the labourers as a woman as far removed from being *"a respectable married woman"* (143) as possible.

When Stacey goes to Buckle's apartment, however, the fantasy of a sexual union in the countryside is shattered by the depravity of his life. Buckle's mother is a grotesque former prostitute, living a sensory-deprived drunken existence. With this unaware audience, Stacey willingly submits to Buckle's advances, only to find he is using her in his perverted masturbation fantasy. Rather than connecting physically with him, Stacey is denied any fulfillment or contact: "What he is doing now concerns only himself, his sex open and erect in his hands" (147). As a final rejection of intimacy, Buckle tosses "bus fare" to Stacey, literally and symbolically paying for her "services." Stacey has now become the figure of a prostituted housewife, mirroring to some degree the figure of Buckle's grotesque mother.

This experience of otherness offers Stacey the element of danger and adventure she seeks, but it does not fulfill her need for more meaningful intimate experiences. In this sense, her step outside her customary and repressive life is a dismal failure, but it also signals Stacey's deeper need to explore the areas of her self that she feels are sadly lacking. Her next foray into otherness comes soon thereafter and enacts Stacey's fantasies much more positively.

When Stacey leaves the city for the second time after a fight with Mac about her involvement with Buckle, it is alone, and there is the sense that, despite this being an unplanned trip, she is more determined in her destination, as she pointedly searches out the countryside. Paralleling her trip with

Buckle, Stacey drives fast and recklessly; however, she is now the driver and is more literally in control. When she finally leaves the city, she feels protected from the subsuming nature of urban space. The countryside is a quiet space, a space where she will be alone with herself, however conflicted that self may be: "How good to hear nothing, no voices. . . . How good it feels, no voices. Except yours, Stacey" (158). This is the solitary space she needs to start understanding her troubled life: "You're alone now. You're off duty. Start sorting, brain child" (159).

After her escape from the city, she comes into contact with a much younger man named Luke Venturi, who invites her into his A-frame house—the structural type implying something elemental, the beginning, as does a book that she sees in his living room, an "illustrated child's ABC" (163)—and it is here that Luke draws out Stacey's true voice, providing her with the venue for the expression of her own more basic emotions. The house and book work as metaphors to describe her personal journey to the more elemental self, and Luke becomes her facilitator. Luke's surname reflects the word "venture," which describes well Stacey's move into the world of emotional expression,[16] and it reinforces the sense of stepping outside the normal sphere of existence. Recognizing her disturbed state and legitimizing it, one of the first things he asks her is "The bad news. What's with you?" (164). When she breaks down in tears soon thereafter, Luke also legitimizes her expression of sorrow, responding to her automatic apology— "I'm sorry I'm sorry"—with, "It's okay, Stacey, you don't have to be sorry. It hurts? . . . Well go ahead and bawl. No shame in that" (165).

As well as valorizing Stacey's emotional life, Luke also pointedly prompts her to step away from her constrained life: "Come out. From wherever you're hiding yourself" (167). On her second visit, he continues to act as a facilitator for her emotions by asking her, "What scares you?" (178), despite her fears that her troubles are boring. Allowed to articulate her troubles, Stacey feels a connectedness with Luke through the seemingly simple—but elusive to her—act of communication.

From this moment of connection, so unlike her recent experiences with Mac, comes a moment of intimacy—through sex—with Luke. Here, too, the differences with Mac's behaviour are stark. Where Mac "makes hate" with her, she immediately connects with Luke in a sharing scenario: "[S]he takes his sex in her hands and guides it into her. She comes before he does, but she is still there when he reaches it. ... Then he rests on her, and she explores his skin" (187). When they part, Stacey "want[s] to thank him" (188), feeling that her evening has been fulfilling emotionally, as well as physically. Stacey then imagines that life with Luke would be an ideal existence: "I'd like to start again, everything, all of life, start again with someone like you—with you—with everything simpler and clearer" (189). Starting over would equal recuperating from the losses of the past by replacing them, rather than by repairing them, but it is an attractive option nonetheless.[17]

Stacey rejects this option, however, when Luke asks Stacey to leave with him: "Why not, merwoman? You want to get away, don't you? I thought that was the whole point with you" (209). She replies, "If I had two lives, I would" (209). That, of course, is the whole point: she cannot be two things at once. She demonstrates her commitment to dealing with her problems at their root as she realizes she must come to terms with the life she has. When she leaves Luke, Stacey "drives fast, hardly seeing where she is going" (210). The driving once again functions as a metaphor for her life—and the work of mourning—as she still does not know how she will deal with her problems but now "her inner automatic pilot . . . [has] taken over" (210).

It is at this point, however, that her work of mourning shifts into its second movement, for she arrives home to the news of Buckle's death and Mac's grief for him. Stacey becomes reflective rather than reactive here, and her decision to help Mac in his time of need reinforces her rejection of Luke's offer. The work of mourning is more strongly recuperative now, and Stacey is able to realign her connections to the losses she mourns, and, most importantly, the work occurs at home.

In this scene, Mac reaches out to Stacey for consolation in his time of emotional need: "holding her not for her need now but for his own" (213). Then, in "a need-admitting sigh," he asks her to drive him to the morgue so he can identify the corpse. While the action of driving[18] is a literal statement of need (he is too emotionally distraught to drive), it is, more importantly, a symbolic expression of his reliance upon her in this moment of emotional difficulty and, thus, reinforces their relationship. After they have returned home, Mac's grief is evident in his physical reactions of vomiting and "lung-wrenching spasms" (216). As part of his mourning, Mac needs to tell the story of his association with Buckle, and to do this he reaches out to Stacey by asking her to be his listener: "Stacey—you don't mind my saying?" (216). In this moment of connection with Mac, Stacey acts as a sort of analyst, prompting Mac to continue his story, just as Luke prompted her. She consoles him—"Sh sh it's all right" (217)—and prompts: "What was it?"; "Go on—say it"; "Say it" (218). Then, mirroring Luke's question, "What scares you, merwoman?" (178), she asks, "Mac—what bugs you?" (219). A sign of Stacey's renewed perspective on her domestic life comes after she and Mac return from the ill-fated Richalife party and she dreams that "*The place is a prison but not totally so*" (235), indicating that the renovated emotional connection with Mac has caused her to revise her view of her repressed life.

Another moment of revision occurs after Stacey's aborted

participation in the peace march. She considers her abandonment of the cause—"I might as well have seen it through. For
what, though? It's like church—you think maybe if you go, the
faith will be given, but it isn't. It has to be there already in you,
I guess" (252)—showing her acceptance of the fact that she
cannot change her essential *self*: there is no magic formula for
changing her life. After the march, Stacey considers her relationship with Luke and accepts her association with him, but
also her ultimate rejection of his offer:

> —you showed me where I belonged, when you said
> *What can't you leave?* I guess I should be grateful. I *am*
> grateful. . . . For the way you talked to me and held me
> for a while—that's why I'm grateful. I said unspokenly
> Help and you didn't turn away. You faced me and
> touched me. You were gentle. (252-53)

At this point, she makes her strongest statement about the
choices she has made in her work of mourning as she
acknowledges her commitment to coming to a new understanding of her mourning. She addresses Luke in her
thoughts: "Even if you'd been older, or I'd been younger and
free, it wouldn't have turned out any simpler with you than it
is with Mac. I didn't see that at one time, but I see it now"
(253). She is now more accepting of the notion that she must
face her problems head-on rather than abandoning them to
start life anew.

Stacey then returns to a phrase she contemplated earlier in
the novel, "pre-mourning," where she was chastised by the
instructor of her night course for mourning the state of the
world. In the juxtaposition of images in this brief moment,
Laurence signals the significant changes that have occurred in
Stacey's thinking about her emotions of loss. Stacey begins by
writing "*No Pre-Mourning*" on a piece of paper from "the
notebook she uses for shopping lists" (253). She tapes this

note above the kitchen sink, presumably as a constant reminder to not allow herself to suffer the feelings of loss she faced earlier in the book. The scene is overtly domestic, and the location of the sign by the sink signals her acceptance of her domesticity, as does the origin of the piece of paper. As Stacey is now in an evaluative rather than reactive mode, she "Stands for a while and looks at it" (253). Juxtaposing this scene of domestic control[19] is the newspaper image of the mourning woman in a "far city . . . holding the dead child" (253-54). The woman is clearly in deep emotional pain: "The woman's mouth open wide—a sound of unbearability but rendered in silence by the camera clicking. Only the zero mouth to be seen, noiselessly proclaiming the gone-early child" (254). This image of the woman who visibly suffers but whose grief goes unheard causes Stacey to re-evaluate her position. At this point she reflects that she "cannot recall what it is that might have been meant by *Pre*" (254). She reinterprets pre-mourning as mourning, as if to say that the amount and type of loss we encounter in the world are so great that it is reasonable to mourn the world as one would a death. In effect, this kind of mourning does not come before other types of mourning: it is not "pre" anything. We are surrounded by loss, and recognition of this fact is the only form of consolation possible. We cannot avoid mourning the world, she is saying, so we must accept our emotions of loss as the only means of coping.

This realization is followed by Stacey's firmest statement of acceptance of herself when she recognizes, a few pages later, that she needs to accept who she is and that her efforts should focus on the things she can change: "It would be nice if we were different people but we are not different people. We are ourselves and we are sure as hell not going to undergo some total transformation at this point" (263-64).

The final event in Stacey's work of mourning is the near

death of her son Duncan, who almost drowns in the sea. In this scene, the symbolism of water—and nature generally—as positive is reversed. The water, previously comforting, is now an instrument of death: "The sea pours from his nostrils. His mouth is open, and his eyes. But he is not seeing anything and he does not seem to be breathing" (266). Rather than swimming gracefully as she used to, Stacey "flounders through the water" (266). While she does save Duncan by pulling him from the water, Stacey fails in being the all-knowing mother-figure here, as she does not know how to proceed thereafter: "She cannot think what to do. She cannot seem to think at all" (266). She ineptly "pushes down on the place where she thinks his lungs are" (266). She ineffectively screams, "*Duncan! You've got to be all right*" (267). She only manages to send Ian off to call Mac and to summon help. A lifeguard arrives to perform artificial respiration, and soon Mac arrives, too. It is, in fact, Ian's summoning of the lifeguard that saves Duncan, and not any specific action that Stacey performed. Through this experience, Stacey learns that she cannot be everything to her children; other forces must intervene to help them through the crises they will encounter in the world. The next time she takes the children to the beach, she shows acceptance and understanding of this as "she makes herself not move" (271) when Duncan goes down to the water. A mother, she concludes, cannot be fully responsible for the dangers of the world, and there will be limits to what can be reasonably expected of her.

At the end of the novel, Stacey has clearly moved beyond the crisis of identity that plagued her and that was precipitated by her inability to deal with loss: "I was wrong to think of the trap as the four walls. It's the world. The truth is that I haven't been Stacey Cameron for one hell of a long time now. Although in some ways I'll always be her, because that's how I started out" (276). While she has clearly changed over the course of the novel, the struggle has been hard-fought and has been indicative of the dangers of living in the modern world. Through her work of mourning, Stacey is somewhat consoled in the face of the troubled world, but the larger conclusion she reaches is that complete consolation may be an unattainable goal. To accept that fact provides, paradoxically, its own consolation, but it also acknowledges the ever-present nature of loss and the fact that to live with it rather than to be subsumed by it is the only option. Stacey finds solace in the realization that grieving is a normal part of her life, and acceptance of this knowledge is what makes loss bearable, thus bringing the novel to a positive conclusion.

With *The Fire-Dwellers*, Laurence ends her contemplation of the constraints placed upon the articulation of emotion by forces outside her protagonists. The general pattern of the work of mourning in the first three novels has been similar in that each protagonist struggled to articulate grief, began mourning unself-consciously, and then finally completed her grieving with full self-awareness. In the next two books, Laurence turns her attention to questions of creativity. She is interested in exploring the links between the articulation of mourning and text-creation, and thus her focus shifts away from the inner struggles of her characters to the artistic modes employed in the creation of the textual work of mourning.

CHAPTER FOUR

"REST BEYOND THE RIVER":
MOURNING IN *A BIRD IN THE HOUSE*

With *A Bird in the House*,[1] published in 1970, Laurence shifts her attention away from the struggles of characters for whom mourning is conflicted, and for whom the work of mourning is ultimately performed under difficult conditions. For Vanessa MacLeod, the protagonist and narrator of this book, and for Morag Gunn, who fulfills the same role in the final novel in the Manawaka series, *The Diviners*, mourning is inextricably linked to the writing of narrative. Rather than fighting with themselves, as well as the world around them, to articulate their constrained grief, as in the cases of Hagar, Rachel, and Stacey, Vanessa and Morag put their efforts into contemplating the best way to work out their mourning textually. Thus, the shape taken by the work of mourning as an aesthetic product is central to *A Bird in the House* and *The Diviners*.

One of the key issues raised by Laurence in *A Bird in the House* is not only how mourning can be represented in textual form, but also how representation itself—the act of writing—is a process of mourning and a functional activity. Laurence utilizes structural and formal concerns implicitly to raise notions of how mourning can be an ordering and organizing activity; in essence, she queries issues of what shape the expression of grief through writing can take. Paralleling these functional concerns are the thematics of Vanessa's narrative, for Vanessa explores the deaths of all the important family members in her past and the mourning activities of the surviving members. All the characters in *A Bird in the House* mourn to some degree, and the book is a wide-ranging exploration of the differences in individual mourning. Vanessa's exploration in her text of these death-related activities can be seen as a means for her to more effectively understand how she herself mourns loss. This book, then, can be conceived as a text that shows how an individual mourns by writing a narrative and as a text that shows how an individual learns to mourn.

Readers of *A Bird in the House* have noted the importance of notions of shaping, ordering, and consciously forming memories—by the narrator and protagonist Vanessa MacLeod—into a carefully structured narrative. Literary critic Arnold Davidson points out that "Vanessa marks—and retrospectively maps—her course to self-determination. In effect, she frees herself psychologically by remembering a place she earlier left physically and by then restructuring or re-creating those memories into meaningful stories."[2] While the ordering and structuring aspects of Vanessa's creative activities in composing her narrative have been identified and explored to some extent in critical responses, the impulses that drive Vanessa's narrative-creation have received little attention. Vanessa's creative activities are catalyzed by a need to come to terms with serious losses in her life. *A Bird in the House* is an exploration of themes of death and mourning and of the role of representing these themes artistically.

In *A Bird in the House*, Vanessa is occupied with constructing a narrative that offers her a sense of consolation in relation to the deaths she has faced in her life. She composes a work of mourning that explores feelings of loss that involve engagement between narrator and reader. Jon Kertzer identifies just such an engagement when he discusses the sense of resolution or consolation that reader and character achieve at the end of *A Bird in the House*. While he does not place his view of resolution within the discourses of work, his assessment of the structural significance of this moment in the book is insightful: "the book ends with a feeling of momentary completion rather than of finality, a feeling that depends on the reader as much as on Vanessa. Both character and reader must feel satisfied."[3]

As with the other novels in the Manawaka series, *A Bird in the House* subtly employs the tradition of elegy as an intertext. In conventional elegy the elegist self-reflexively engages with issues related to the aesthetic creation—the act itself as process—of the poem, commenting on the emotional origins of the impulse to write a text of mourning.[4] Further, Laurence engages the convention of the procession of mourners, so common to elegy, from which the elegist can learn about grief and its effective expression. This is akin to how Vanessa learns about mourning by observing members of her family struggle, some with success and others without, in their attempts to come to grips with loss.[5]

Formally, *A Bird in the House* is divided into eight separate stories, which, nonetheless, have a coherence and unity that approach that of a novel.[6] Structurally, the text makes up a series of intertwined recollections about growing up in Manawaka that are told retrospectively by a mature Vanessa.

The narrative is framed by six paragraphs set off from the text of the final story, "Jericho's Brick Battlements," at the very end of the book. This section contextualizes the narrative the reader has just encountered and serves as a self-reflexive commentary on the purpose of the narrator's storytelling. This section is important in identifying Vanessa's narrative as a work of mourning—a text written because an individual needs to mourn and is the result of the person's mourning actions (in this case, creative activities). A work of mourning is defined by literary critic Karen E. Smythe in *Figuring Grief: Gallant, Munro, and the Poetics of Elegy* as being "a specific example of the ways in which we use stories to shape our lives, our experiences";[7] by writing her work of mourning, Vanessa orders the experiences that have shaped her in life and thus gains insight into her sense of identity. The framing sections also reinforce the sense that the stories Vanessa tells are her means of moving through a liminal state initiated by the return to Manawaka. The narrative closure implied by her driving away from the Brick House in the last line of the novel indicates the end of her liminality.

Kertzer identifies *A Bird in the House* as a confessional memoir, as a text that "is a sustained act of memory that aims at a totality of vision and judgement." The memoir functions through the process of confession—"that is, honest self-revelation"—and allows Vanessa "to see life whole."[8] The form of the confessional memoir is particularly conducive to an examination of identity—one of the basic activities of mourning—and to an understanding of personal development. As a creative endeavour, the memoir form is favourable to self-discovery: "Vanessa discovers that remembrance, confession, and personal identity all depend on story-telling."[9]

Laurence places great importance on the notion of setting things in order in *A Bird in the House* and acknowledges in this book that such ordering is an entirely artificial means of coming to terms with loss in life. It is, however, the only way for her character to understand her past and to make sense of it in her present-day life. The first and last stories of *A Bird in the House*, "The Sound of the Singing" and "Jericho's Brick Battlements," frame the retrospective narrative Vanessa constructs in "To Set Our House in Order," "A Bird in the House," and "The Mask of the Bear," and have the function of offering a commentary on the roles of mourning, memory, and the conscious activity of storytelling.

A Bird in the House opens with Vanessa's contemplation, in "The Sound of the Singing," of the significance of her Grandfather Connor's house to her own life. As she asserts, "That house in Manawaka is the one which, more than any other, I carry with me" (11). Later, in concluding the paragraph, Vanessa thinks of the house as a "massive monument" (11). While the rest of "The Sound of the Singing" introduces her Grandfather Connor and his tyrannical influence on his family, the notion of why and how the house becomes a monument—and importantly, to whom and to what—is left for the closing story of the book, "Jericho's Brick Battlements." At the very end of this story Vanessa returns to the notion of monuments, making possible a larger conception, by the reader, of structure and function in *A Bird in the House*, for it is here that the narrator comes full circle in her storytelling by paralleling the opening description of the Brick House with another, quite different, description. This is a depiction that sets memory as a priority over the actual physical object in the pursuit of consolation. Since the preceding narrative is entirely made up of memories, Vanessa, at the end of *A Bird in the House*, is avowing a mourning practice that relies not on the real, but on memory rendered fictionally. For Vanessa, it is not the physical presence of the Brick House that exists as the monument to her grandfather, but the memory of it, and the active recollection of the house and all that transpired within its walls, that becomes monumental, along with the subsequent rendering of those memories artistically. While Vanessa disavows her Grandfather Connor's grave as his memorial ("I did not look at Grandfather Connor's grave. There was no need. It was not his monument" [191]), she also minimizes the significance of the physical edifice itself. As Vanessa remarks, the house has passed out of the family's hands and no longer retains the characteristics that defined it as the Brick House of the Connors of old:

> The caragana hedge was unruly. No one had trimmed it properly that summer. The house had been lived in by strangers for a long time. I had not thought it would hurt me to see it in other hands, but it did. I wanted to tell them to trim their hedges, to repaint the windowframes, to pay heed to repairs. I had feared and fought the old man, yet he proclaimed himself in my veins. But it was their house now, whoever they were, not ours, not mine. (191)

The narrator asserts that she only "looked at it for a moment" (191), and yet the house acts as a focalizing agent in the opening story and remains central as an image throughout *A Bird in the House*. The adjectives used to describe the house reflect an artistically refracted vision of the building and not an objective pictorial representation. As Vanessa writes, "[the house] was plain as the winter turnips in its root cellar, sparsely windowed as some crusader's embattled fortress in a heathen wilderness, its rooms in a perpetual gloom except in the brief height of summer" (11). Furthermore, Vanessa's choice of metaphors imbues the description of the house with a symbolism that reflects the characteristics ascribed to her Grandfather Connor later in the story, adding to the impression that the significance of the house lies not in the physical presence of the object, but in the artistic representation—one that can imbue the house with some of the life once contained within its walls.

The whole last section of "Jericho's Brick Battlements" is a proclamation of the importance of memory, rather than the presence of the actual in mourning, and of the significance of representing the past artistically. Vanessa makes a key statement here about her mourning, since, evidently, the dead are always beyond physical recovery; but, for the mourning subject, there must be some means of recovering the loss in a meaningful way—which, in Vanessa's case, is through artistic representation. Everything Vanessa encounters during her visit to Manawaka after a twenty-year absence is without concrete significance—like the Brick House itself. As she points out, without the presence of family members in Manawaka, "there was nothing to take me there any more" (190). Seeing her parents' graves causes Vanessa to reflect not upon them directly, but upon herself and her inheritance: "I realized from the dates on the stone that my father had died when he was the same age as I was now. I remembered saying things to my children that my mother had said to me, the clichés of affection, perhaps inherited from her mother" (190). The references to her parents and their graves are fleeting, just like Vanessa's trip back to Manawaka. It is left up to the artistic representation of her parents' lives, in the stories that make up *A Bird in the House*, to act as true memorials to their existence. The strategic placement of Vanessa's return to Manawaka and her visit to her parents' graves at the very end of the book underscores the role of mourning—of working through loss—in *A Bird in the House* and comments implicitly on the function of the preceding narrative in Vanessa's life. Vanessa reflects upon the deaths that have touched her most closely and contextualizes the telling of the stories.

In the stories Vanessa tells in her narrative, there are many examples of individuals who are in the process of mourning a loss, and she is provided in her young life with numerous occasions for observing others in their grief, a first-hand

experience of how people react to death—something that ultimately affects the way she, too, grieves. In this way, *A Bird in
the House* is a narrative about how an individual learns to
mourn by seeing how others mourn.

In a sequence dealing with Grandmother MacLeod that
begins with "To Set Our House in Order," Vanessa learns
about undue attachments to the dead and how such attachments can have harmful effects on those still living. The story
shifts between her own growing awareness that death can have
an effect on her life and her observations of how others deal
with grief. She sees her Grandmother MacLeod appear to be
in denial of her son Roderick's death many years ago, but she
also sees that her father struggles in his own private way to
deal with his brother's tragic demise. The young Vanessa,
depicted in the story, has difficulty understanding the complexity of her grandmother's grief, but the older narrating
Vanessa is able to take a more objective stance. The work of
mourning she composes becomes a contemplation on the difficulties of grieving effectively as well as an attempt to understand how her younger self became increasingly aware of how
loss affected members of her family. This is an important contemplation in terms of the mourning the narrating Vanessa is
carrying out, for her larger aim is to work through the emotional moment that initially catalyzed the composition of stories about her past.

"To Set Our House in Order," then, opens with the news
that Vanessa's mother's pregnancy is not going well, and this
becomes Vanessa's first realization of mortality. In large part,
the story is about how Vanessa comes to learn a little more
about the vagaries of life and death, and of how tenuous and
unpredictable life actually is. Her Grandmother MacLeod's
still unconsoled grief for her son Roderick, who was killed
during the war, gives Vanessa some insight into the difficulties
of letting go of the dead. As Vanessa attempts to come to

terms with the fact that her mother may die in childbirth, her
grandmother tries to placate her by citing her perception of
her own experience—a rational and ordered vision of mourning the death of Roderick. She instructs, "What happens is
God's will. The Lord giveth, and the Lord taketh away" (48).
These harsh, pragmatic words appall Vanessa, but they make
sense within Grandmother MacLeod's own understanding of
the world. As she points out, "When your Uncle Roderick
got killed . . . I thought that I would die. But I didn't die,
Vanessa" (48). What she preaches is stoic acceptance of the
tragic and chaotic events of life. However, her own practice
refutes the lessons she hopes to pass along to her grandchild.
Grandmother MacLeod's inability to deal with the memories
of Roderick result in a stultifying atmosphere in her life and
house—an atmosphere that seriously affects her relationship
with her other son, Vanessa's father—and stands in stark
counterpoint to her feeling that "God loves Order. . . . God
loves Order—he wants each one of us to set our house in
order" (49).

Grandmother MacLeod's bedroom is an example of how
she has kept her life, essentially, stuck in the past, a sort of per-
manent liminal state. It is a stultifying place, out of bounds for
Vanessa, that has been kept sterile and clear of the disorder a
healthy daily life would cause:

> [My] presence, if not actually forbidden, was not
> encouraged . . . [in] Grandmother MacLeod's bedroom,
> with its stale and old-smelling air, the dim reek of medi-
> cines and lavender sachets. Here resided her mono-
> grammed dresser silver, brush and mirror, nail-buffer
> and button hook and scissors, none of which must even
> be fingered by me now. (47)

This same stale room is where the memories of Roderick
are kept alive and somehow never let go: "Here, too, were the
silver-framed photographs of Uncle Roderick—as a child, as a

boy, as a man in his Army uniform" (47). And later, in the title story, Vanessa thinks of her grandmother as "sleeping with her mouth open in her enormous spool bed surrounded by half a dozen framed photos of Uncle Roderick and only one of my father" (103). It is almost as if, with the death of Roderick, Grandmother MacLeod's life, too, has become static. The sense of lifelessness extends to the house as a whole, as it has an atmosphere of being stopped in time, that denies the effects of the currents of daily life. Vanessa remembers the house as being "like a museum, full of dead and meaningless objects, vases and gilt-framed pictures and looming furniture, all of which had to be dusted and catered to for reasons which everyone had forgotten" (78). In another memory, Vanessa thinks of the house in terms of death, as opposed to reflecting the lives that the dead lived:

> The unseen presences . . . I knew to be those of every person, young or old, who had ever belonged to the house and had died, including Uncle Roderick who got killed on the Somme, and the baby who would have been my sister if only she had managed to come to life. (46)

While Grandmother MacLeod's sensibility imposes order on the deaths in her life, the order does not provide consolation; nor is it particularly effective. Essentially, Grandmother MacLeod's order is one that unintentionally excludes everyone but herself. For example, when Beth's baby is finally born, Grandmother MacLeod's sense of order dictates that the boy be called Roderick to ensure her son's memory is passed on. While her wishes seem reasonable enough, she does not ever consider that Ewen, too, has suffered because of the loss of his brother. For her, there is only one appropriate action, one sanctioned response to death. It is an order that does not suit everyone equally. Vanessa can appreciate the grief her grandmother feels—"All at once, her feelings for that unknown dead man became a reality for me" (57)—but she also realizes that grief can be harmful if it is allowed to consume those who remain alive.

At the conclusion of "To Set Our House in Order," Vanessa contemplates order and disorder, for she has seen that order does not necessarily represent the best solution to events, and she has seen that unpredictable events are a part of daily life. She ruminates: "I thought of the accidents that might easily happen to a person—or, of course, might not happen, might happen to somebody else" (60). And she concludes, later, "I felt that whatever God might love in this world, it was certainly not order" (61). And yet, these words are the thoughts of the young Vanessa, and not the older narrating person. Literary critic Michael Darling points out that, "in giving order to her own life by retelling the events of her childhood, Vanessa learns that seemingly obvious differences conceal deeper affinities, and that an apparently rigid order may be only a flimsy structure hiding a chaotic turmoil."[10] Indeed, it is the kind of order imposed on events that is important here for Vanessa. The implicit rejection of her grandmother's order is a significant step in gaining an awareness of what will work for her own mourning in her specific frame of reference, which, of course, is to work through the emotions she feels upon seeing her parents' graves and her grandfather's house.

Three scenes, in "The Mask of the Bear" and "A Bird in the House," dealing with processions or parades, reinforce the learning aspect of Vanessa's storytelling in *A Bird in the House*. The first, presented in "The Mask of the Bear," involves the death scenes Vanessa writes in her story about an Egyptian heroine. For Vanessa, "The death scenes had an undeniable appeal, a sombre splendour, with (as it said in Ecclesiastes) the mourners going about the streets and all the daughters of music brought low" (66). Here, she sees the procession of mourners in a romanticized sense and is concerned about aesthetic effect: she feels the procession would add to its effect. Later, in "The Mask of the Bear," after her Grandmother Connor has died, Vanessa looks to Ecclesiastes to help her shape "her own funeral service for my grandmother" (82). With different aesthetic aims, however, the elements that she so liked now fail to offer her consolation: "I intended to read the part about the mourners going about the streets. . . . But I got stuck on the first few lines, because it seemed to me, frighteningly, that they were being spoken in my grandmother's mild voice" (82).

The failure of imagination to provide consolation is linked with Vanessa's refusal to attend the Remembrance Day parade (a form of procession, of course) in the next story in the book, "A Bird in the House." In the opening pages, Vanessa justifies her refusal by signalling the pointlessness of the parade, as she tells her father: "They look silly. . . . Marching like that" (90). When she probes her father about his brother Roderick's death during the Great War, she quickly realizes the significance of the parade:

> Unexpectedly, that day came into intense being for me. He had had to watch his own brother die, not in the antiseptic calm of some hospital, but out in the open, the stretches of mud I had seen in his snapshots. . . . I looked at my father with a kind of horrified awe, and then I began to cry. . . . now I needed him to console me for this unwanted glimpse of the pain he had once known. (91)

In the contemplation of these three scenes in her storytelling, Vanessa retrospectively learns that the structures of mourning that offer consolation are dependent on context. The procession in Ecclesiastes does not ring true in memorializing her grandmother, but she understands the consolatory function of the Remembrance Day parade when she witnesses her father's pain. By inscribing these scenes in her stories, Vanessa repeats the intentions of her younger self when she wrote of the Egyptian heroine, only now her aesthetic aims are to fulfill the requirements of the work of mourning.

In "The Mask of the Bear," Vanessa experiences for the first time the grief of someone close to her, and she sees here that an individual's mourning does not always manifest as one would expect. Not only does Vanessa have her own first experience of losing a close family member, but she also witnesses her Grandfather Connor's grief at the death of his wife. Early in "The Mask of the Bear," the narrator remembers her image of death and mourning as it is represented in the stories she writes. In her stories, death is romanticized and depicted as an event closer to glory than misery. For Vanessa, "death and love seemed regrettably far from Manawaka," but, as she finds out soon enough in the events that transpire in her life, these events are not at all as she has envisioned them. Later in the story, the focus shifts to the death of Grandmother Connor. When her grandfather explains to her what has happened, Vanessa at first is more shocked by Grandfather Connor's reaction to the death than to the loss itself—for Vanessa has never seen this kind of emotion in him before: "As I gazed at him, unable to take in the significance of what he has said, he did a horrifying thing. He gathered me into the relentless grip of his arms. He bent low over me, and sobbed against the cold skin of my face" (79). At this stage, Vanessa is still unsure of exactly what the loss of a family member represents, and incredulity reigns in her mind: "I still could not believe that anyone I cared about could really die," she thinks; and "I did not fully realize yet that Grandmother Connor would never move around this house again, preserving its uncertain peace somehow" (80). What she does gain, however, is an insight into the nature of death and into the pain that accompanies loss: "I had not known at all that a death would be like this, not only one's own pain, but the almost unbearable knowledge of that other pain which could not be reached or lessened" (80).

Vanessa's exploration of her father's death in the fourth story in the volume, "A Bird in the House," offers insight into another mode of mourning loss, one informed by religion. Like her Grandmother MacLeod's stoic form of ordering death-related experience, this religious form of response (which is, after all, another way of ordering experience) is found to be antipathetic to Vanessa, too. Running through the story are notions of what sort of afterlife the deceased can expect to encounter, one version of which is rendered by Noreen, the hired girl. Noreen's vision of life after death includes both heaven and hell, places that she

> had an intimate and detailed knowledge of. . . . She not only knew what they looked like—she even knew how big they were. Heaven was seventy-seven thousand miles square and it had four gates, each one made out of a different kind of precious jewel. The Pearl Gate, the Topaz Gate, the Amethyst Gate, the Ruby Gate—Noreen could reel them all off.
> Hell was one hundred and ninety million miles deep and was in perpetual darkness, like a cave or under the sea. Even the flames (this was the awful thing) *did not give off any light.* (96)

Yet this version of the afterlife is alien to Vanessa's own religious upbringing, and offers her no conceptual possibility. The more familiar words of a church hymn seem to indicate the possibility of an afterlife at this point in the story. The words include the phrase "Rest beyond the river," which seems to Vanessa more appropriate for Grandmother Connor than Noreen's version of Heaven. Vanessa asserts, "She had believed in Heaven, but I did not think that rest beyond the river was quite what she had in mind. To think of her in Noreen's flashy Heaven, though—that was even worse" (100). Indeed, Vanessa's conception of a heaven where her grandmother could rest in peace mirrors her conception of her grandmother's character:

> Someplace where nobody ever got annoyed or had to be
> smoothed down and placated, someplace where there
> were never any family scenes—that would have suited
> my Grandmother Connor. Maybe she wouldn't have
> minded a certain amount of rest beyond the river, at that.
> (100)

When Vanessa's father dies, however, she finds that a
response to death guided by religion offers her no consolation.
When Vanessa remembers the visits by the local church minister to her mother after the death, her memory is formulated
in language that reflects the negative aspects of the experience
and not any potential good that might have resulted:

> What I thought chiefly was that he would speak of the
> healing power of prayer, and all that, and it would be
> bound to make my mother cry again. And in fact, it hap-
> pened in just that way, but when it actually came, I could
> not protect her from this assault. I could only sit there
> and pray my own prayer, which was that he would go
> away quickly. (103–104)

Vanessa rejects the prayer—the ordered means of grieving
that Reverend McKee offers; and, indeed, her choice of the
word "assault" to describe his advice effectively represents her
view of his coping strategies. After her experiences with the
way organized religion deals with death, Vanessa rejects out-
right the notion of an afterlife. She feels that her father "is not
in Heaven, because there is no Heaven" (105). And the words
from the hymn, "Rest beyond the river," no longer have the
influence on her they originally had: "I knew now what that
meant. It meant Nothing. It meant only silence, forever" (105).

An examination of the funerals represented in the text
reveals much about Vanessa's relationship both to recreating
the past and to coming to terms with the dead. Similar to her
opinion of Grandmother MacLeod's reliance on rigid notions

of order, which represent a kind of tradition, Vanessa has little regard for the effect of the ordered forms of mourning ritual—namely, the funeral.

In "Jericho's Brick Battlements," Vanessa comments on funerals by remarking on the "Bizarre cruelty of such rituals" (188). While a number of people died during her formative years, Vanessa never actually attended a funeral until her Grandfather Connor's when she was twenty. This is in large part due to the prevailing notion that children should not be exposed to such rituals and should be protected from death. Vanessa reflects upon how her grandfather's funeral service shapes and orders the memory of his life, but also imposes a legitimized version of events:

> What funeral could my grandfather have been given except the one he got? The sombre hymns were sung, and he was sent to his Maker by the United Church minister, who spoke, as expected, of the fact that Timothy Connor had been one of Manawaka's pioneers. He had come from Ontario to Manitoba by Red River steamer, and he had walked from Winnipeg to Manawaka, earning his way by shoeing horses. After some years as a blacksmith, he had enough money to go into the hardware business. Then he had built his house. It had been the first brick house in Manawaka. (189)

What is particularly striking about this narrative is that it is a sparing account of a man's life and resembles most closely the form of the newspaper obituary. The bare essentials provide all the important facts, but do not give much in terms of what the man was actually like. The conventional summary of his life does little, in fact, to convey what kind of person he was. In telling her own stories, Vanessa rewrites these conventional forms of summing up a person's life, and, through artistry, she shows how another way can be more effective in getting at the true essence of a life.

Contrasting the passage about Grandfather Connor's funeral is an imagined reconstruction of his brother Dan's funeral. While Vanessa knows the funeral could not have been as she envisions it, she decides the imagined version is more appropriate and does greater justice to the man's life—which, in the end, does not amount to much in terms of a conventional summation:

> Dan had never ceased being a no-good, a natural-born stage Irishman, who continued even when he was senile to sing rebel songs. For years Grandfather Connor had virtually supported him. His funeral must have been quiet and impoverished, but in my head I had always imagined the funeral he ought to have had. His coffin should have been borne by a hayrack festooned with green ribbons and drawn by six snorting black stallions, and all the cornets and drums of the town band should have broken loose with "Glory O, Glory O, to the Bold Fenian Men." (188)

Anything but conventional, this imagined funeral does justice to the soul of the man, rather than to the quantifiable life. Such an approach informs Vanessa's own practice in remembering the dead.

A Bird in the House is very much focussed on Vanessa's memories of her grandfather, and her narrative can be seen as a rewriting of the spare account of his life that she encountered at his funeral. This account did not inspire in Vanessa any emotional response to Grandfather Connor's death: "I could not cry. I wanted to, but I could not" (189). Later, when Vanessa observes his body—"after the accepted custom"—the sense that she is not emotionally engaged in the funeral service is underscored: "I was not sorry that he was dead. I was only surprised" (189). It is only many years later that Vanessa can begin to explore the relationship she had with her grandfather, and the first step is to acknowledge that his influence was integral in forming the person she has now become.

Vanessa reflects at the end of the book that "I had feared and fought the old man, yet he proclaimed himself in my veins" (191). Her narrative, then, seeks to find a way that allows her to understand—and accept—how her grandfather "proclaims" himself in her veins. Vanessa's narrative in *A Bird in the House* becomes a text that mourns her grandfather's life and death, as well as a work that mourns the other important losses of her life. Mourning is a process that implicitly involves the questioning of social structures and shaping forces, and Vanessa's practice in the text embodies the definition. She questions and rejects traditional forms of mourning because they have not fulfilled her emotional needs, but she also constructs her own manner of grieving from the experiences she has had, and she finds that, through creative means, she is able to mourn the losses of her life.

In the next novel, *The Diviners*, Laurence continues with her contemplation of the link between artistic creation and mourning. She adds sophistication to her conception of the work of mourning as a text by the self-reflexive commentary of her narrator and protagonist, Morag Gunn. Morag is clearly identified as a writer, where Vanessa is so only by implication, and she more clearly addresses and theorizes the process of creating the narrative she is writing than Vanessa does.

CHAPTER FIVE

THE DIVINERS
AND THE WORK OF MOURNING

In *The Diviners*, as in *A Bird in the House*, Laurence focusses her attention on the role and function of death in fictional narrative. Of all the Manawaka novels, *The Diviners* is the most interesting in this regard because it is here that Laurence explores with the most complexity the role and function of mourning and the nature of the creative project. She examines the inspiration of the creative act, querying the genesis of the aesthetic enterprise and the connection between the emotions involved in grieving and the production of narrative. While Morag Gunn's creativity results from the contemplation of, and reaction to, loss, as does Vanessa's in *A Bird in the House*, Laurence theorizes issues of writing more overtly in *The Diviners* in an attempt to come to a fuller understanding of the relation between loss and creativity.

Much of *The Diviners* is comprised of a novel that Morag writes: Laurence employs a frame-text and embedded narrative structure in the novel; the embedded text is the novel, and the frame-text provides metatextual commentary on the context of its production. Central to her created narrative are the experiences of death that she relates from her past, which she now revisits and memorializes by inscribing them into her text. Her narrative is ordered specifically by five separate experiences of death, four of them in her remembered past and one in the present of the narrative, and each instance of death corresponds to one of the major divisions in the text. These encounters with death are represented as death scenes, and, by her deliberate writing of them into her text, Morag instills the scenes with narrative function: the death scenes become textual elements that order the narrative, but also mark the events that have most affected her life and are major turning points. As narrative-ordering agents, then, the death experiences reinforce the function of Morag's narrative as a work of mourning, for, by placing special emphasis on her experiences, she asserts their importance in respect to the rest of her life. The novel she writes is epic in scope, reaching back to her childhood and extending to the present moment of her life.

Morag's narrative can be considered as a variation on the *bildungsroman*. Nora Stovel refines the generic categorization of the novel as *bildungsroman* by asserting that *The Diviners* is most accurately termed a *kunstlerroman*, "chronicling the development of an artist."[1] A further delineation is possible: perhaps the word *thanatosroman* (to my knowledge this term has never been employed before) would be appropriate. This term does not deny the appellation *kunstlerroman* because the writing or figuring of death is imperative to the workings of such a text. A *thanatosroman* could be defined as the learning of a life through an exposure to death—the development of the individual through an understanding of death *through* the figuring of death.

Morag's labour of mourning begins with her contemplation of her daughter Pique's departure in the opening sequence of the novel, acting as a catalyst for her emotions and causing the reopening of old wounds and scars that have not yet fully healed. In Morag's case, it quickly becomes evident she has yet to mourn fully and thus understand the effects of the premature deaths of her biological father and mother. The event of Pique's departure is similar in seriousness to the birth of a child, a marriage, or the death of a family member: it is the kind of change that throws into question issues of identity and that forces re-examination of the self. Morag's return to the photos of her childhood, her "totems," demonstrates her need to re-examine her *self* in relation to her roots.[2] The departure of Pique, then, has a doubly unsettling effect on Morag's life: it is the cause of immediate feelings of loss, and it brings old pain to the surface of her consciousness—old pain that this time demands to be dealt with.

Initially, Pique's departure results in Morag's being thrust into an uncertain and liminal psychic space, and her (re)actions partake of a liminal moment. Morag finds herself in an in-between psychic moment whereby her everyday world is destabilized so that she feels caught between the past and the future. The imagery of the opening scene of the novel reflects her sense of liminality, for the river is described as flowing "both ways" (11). The liminal space she occupies is doubly uncertain because of the reawakening of the old losses that have yet to be properly mourned. Thus, Pique's departure is only the surface loss Morag suffers, and the death of her parents is the underlying—and the more serious—loss that she faces, followed by the deaths of Christie and Prin, her foster parents. And yet the initial loss Morag feels at Pique's leaving is the catalyst for revisiting the others, and it is what initiates her creative mode. The narrative she writes in response helps her to organize and shape her emotions. Rather than retreat, she now actively and self-consciously engages emotion through writing and creativity.[3]

A critical element of Morag's fictionalizing is the function that the act of creation, as a psychically positive experience, fulfills. Words are not, as Morag says, "magic," but they do offer escape and possibility—the possibility of coping with loss. Words, in the end, do not create the miracle of complete freedom from the losses that have plagued Morag's life, but words do make the understanding of those losses, and the effects they have had on the course of her life, possible. And that, for Morag, is a sort of miracle, after all. Morag comes to this knowledge after she has written most of the "private and fictional words" (477) that make up the novel she is writing throughout *The Diviners*. It is not the product of the writing that produces the understanding, but the action of *doing* the writing, of working out the problems with words—the process of writing itself—that allows emotional release from her psychic burdens: "She would never know whether . . . [her magic tricks] actually worked or not, or to what extent. That wasn't given to her to know. In a sense, it didn't matter. The necessary doing of the thing—that mattered" (477).

The texts Morag constructs out of her grief in *The Diviners*, to borrow critic Esther Rashkin's words about *Babette's Feast*, "function as a vehicle for articulating a fundamental connection between artistic creation and [her] bereavement, between literary inscription and psychic memorialization, and between the production of narrative as an aesthetic enterprise and the creation of art as a life-saving act."[4] Writing is, for Morag, the measure for coping with the loss—both literal and figurative—of Pique as well as with the memories of previous losses brought to immediacy by her departure.

Thus, writing creatively is how Morag moves herself

through her liminal state, and the structure she employs can be directly related to that aesthetic enterprise. As a work of mourning, the novel is carefully organized to reveal the significance of Morag's and Pique's parallel journeys and to frame Morag's own need to mourn the serious losses of her life and all that these losses represent. The novel is divided into five separate sections and further divided into eleven chapters. The first and last sections—titled "The River of Now and Then" and "The Diviners"—literally frame the text and provide a circularity to it by presenting the narrative of Morag and Pique's troubles. Both sections are almost identical in length. The three middle sections deal primarily with the stories Morag tells/creates, but the framing text is prominent throughout as well, intersecting Morag's narrative in each chapter. The individual chapters open with a scene from the frame-text, as well as help to contextualize the need for storytelling.[5] Additionally, Morag inscribes each death scene with corporeal detail, avoiding the denial of the factuality of death and terminal illness that her social world supports and that plagued her experience of her parents' deaths. She also explores the conventional rites associated with death and dying, figuring them in her narrative as depersonalized and in need of individualizing in order to effectively meet the needs of the mourners.

The five death scenes Morag writes into her narrative help her gain important insights into the personal issues related to loss and into the influence of social and cultural matters encompassing death experiences. By figuring, or representing, these deaths Morag works her way through significant issues related to her understanding of death and mourning and their effect on her life. As the object of her narrative is to help her understand her own grief, the telling of each mourning experience has its own significance in relation to her understanding of her work of mourning, thus contributing to it as well as enacting it.

Literary critic Richard Stamelman remarks:

> Images, words, and texts are what we depend on in order to make note of what has passed away. These representations may reflect the past as well as reflect upon it, but they are without the power to re-create the living sensation of that past. . . . The past is irrevocably and irreversibly lost.[6]

Morag, of course, is fully aware of the impossibility of bringing back the dead through representation. She laments not being able to write her parents' death scene, for she feels that even that fleeting moment figured would bring some consolation, but she realizes that, for her, the fictional recreation of a death scene—and even the attempt to—has a consoling function. Mourning, for Morag, is not about noting the failure of language to go beyond the signifier, to reproduce the signified,[7] but, rather, it is to use language as a facilitating agent in the understanding of her relationship to what has been lost. By naming the loss, she feels she can better understand its effect on her life. Thus, the writing of the death scenes becomes an inherently positive activity.

Morag's recollections of death, and specifically the death scenes, depict key moments in her developmental life, punctuating her narrative and representing turning points in her life—one in each major section of the book she writes. The first scene, the death of her parents in the first part of *The Diviners*, "The River of Now and Then," is one she is not allowed to witness, but it is the defining death moment of her life, for it forever alters the course of her existence. The second death scene Morag writes is that of Piquette Tonnerre and her daughter at the Tonnerre shack in the Wachakwa valley, where the physicality of death is brought up close as an undeniable reality in her life, allowing her the graphic experience of the corporeality of death that was previously denied to her

in childhood.[8] The third scene of death involves Prin, her foster mother: by witnessing Prin's death and the funeral rites
thereafter, Morag is jolted into questioning her (false) life with
her husband Brooke, and she makes the life-altering decision
to leave him. The next scene is that of Christie's death: after
that, Morag makes an important life decision because moving
back to Canada affirms her sense of heritage. The scene of
Jules's death is the fifth and final one of the novel. Like the
death scene of her parents, Jules's death takes place in the
framing text of the book and provides a structural and the-
matic comment on Morag's ability to cope with loss.

Literary critic Beatrice Martina Guenther remarks that
"the radicality of the death scene grants it a special, metatextual status in any literary project."[9] As "metatextual" elements
in Morag's text, the death scenes become markers of the structuring of her fictionally represented life, and they have a the-
matic role in marking the changes Morag undergoes in her
understanding of death and consolation. As Paul Hjartarson
notes in "Christie's Real Country," "Whereas the five-year-old
feels both locked out and locked in, frighteningly alone," in the
first death scene, by the final one, Morag "lives in the knowledge not only of death but of comfort given and received."[10]

The first death scene Morag experiences is that of her parents, and it comes at the very early age of five, when she is
ill-equipped to deal with the loss. The deaths also come his-
torically at a time when the factuality of death was denied
children. Morag does not actually witness the deaths, yet they
leave a lasting impression on her that supercedes any later
experience of death. The deaths are figured in the opening
section of the novel as a large void or absence in her life, and
Morag's lack of knowledge and understanding about the way
they died causes a psychic wound for her, which resurfaces
later when she feels the need to try to understand their
relation to her life. Language is the only means of escaping the

utter silence that accompanies their death, yet Morag struggles with articulating the gaps in her knowledge. She can
depict her young self in bewilderment, yearning for the forbidden space of upstairs, where her parents lie in their
sickbeds, but she cannot articulate what she does not know.
This death scene is the most important one for Morag's subsequent development, for it figures an essential, elemental,
absence in her life—one she forever tries to fill. "Death makes
the characters become the absolute and absent cause [in *The
Diviners*]," writes critic Barbara Godard;[11] "The reality of
being is replaced by the reality of saying." Thus, as critic
Méira Cook suggests, Morag's life becomes in part a "quest of
narrative. . . . a quest for a code and a meaning" to fill the ever-
present void of knowledge in her life.[12]

All Morag's memories of her parents are constructed references based on the snapshots of them she has kept over the
years because they "contain a portion of my spirit" (14).
Morag remarks to herself that "*I keep the snapshots not for what
they show but for what is hidden in them*" (14). Thus, her frame
of reference for her parents is entirely an imaginatively constructed one that reinforces the role of creativity in her life.
Contained in the photos is not "real" knowledge of her parents, but only glimpses of what they may have been like. As
Morag looks at the first snapshot of her parents, for example,
all she is able to articulate is a distanced description of the
image as she sees it:

> *The man and woman are standing stiffly on either side of the
> gate. It is a farm gate, very wide, dark metal, and old—as is
> shown by the sagging. The man is not touching the woman,
> but they stand close. She is young, clad in a cotton print dress
> (the pattern cannot be discerned) which appears too large for
> her thin frame.* (14)

The words are those of an objective, impersonal observer,

rather than those of a viewing mediated through actual memory. With the next snapshot, Morag begins to add to the photo, interpreting and elaborating on the images she sees. The picture is of a child sitting with her dog. From the initial objective description, Morag adds to the image self-consciously:

> The dog, as one would not guess from the picture, is called Snap, short for Snapdragon. . . . He would snap at thieves if there were any, but there aren't, ever. . . . Morag's mother is not the sort of mother who yells at kids. She does not whine either. She is like Prin. (15-16)

The final reference to Prin betrays to Morag, and to the reader, that she is adding to what the photo could possibly reveal: "*All this is crazy, of course, and quite untrue. Or maybe true and maybe not. I am remembering myself composing this interpretation, in Christie and Prin's house*" (16). Morag's indeterminacy in ascertaining the truth value of the photo, and of her memories, is important because it underscores the void in her knowledge of her parents.

Constructed from what she perceives of them in the photos, Morag's early memories of her parents are mostly invented. Her memories are idealized versions of her parents, adding to her sense of loss: they are perfect parents, in her mind. She thinks of her mother as a woman who does not yell, and "Her father never minds helping her. He always has time" (16). Her father is constructed (as is her mother) in contrast to the foster parents who take charge of her after the deaths. In her invented memories, Morag's father always "smells warm and good. Clean. Smells of soap and greengrass. Not manure. He never stinks of horseshit, even though he is a farmer" (16). Christie, of course, is like the envelope he gave Morag to keep her snapshots in: he frequently smells "faintly shitlike, faintly like the sweetish ether smell of spoiled fruit" (14)—in large part because of his job as the town refuse collector.

Helen Buss describes Morag's early life as a "childhood paradise"[13] whose loss she later mourns. Thus, Morag never grieves for the actual lost world (as she has no concrete memory of it); rather, she mourns the loss of the perfect world of her imagination. As she thinks, *"I recall looking at the pictures, these pictures, over and over again, each time imagining I remembered a little more"* (17). And then, after she has looked at all the photos of her parents, she remarks to herself, *"And that is the end of the totally invented memories. I can't remember myself actually being aware of inventing them, but it must have happened so. How much later? At Christie's, of course, putting myself to sleep"* (19). Morag's inventions/fictions here serve an early function of consolation, prefiguring her much later and more overt use of fiction as a consoling device.

The underlying truth to all Morag's memories of her parents is that she has no real knowledge of them as people, but rather as meaningless faces and figures in the photos: *"I cannot really remember my parents' faces at all. When I look now at that one snapshot of them, they aren't faces I can relate to anyone I ever knew. It didn't bother me for years and years."* But now, Morag mourns this lack of knowledge, as she thinks, *"Why should it grieve me now? Why do I want them back?"* (19). The answer is that Morag would like to have just one actual, physical, impression of her mother and father, an impression that all the figured, or represented, images cannot make up for. Morag grieves in part because she remembers the imaginary characters of her childhood—"Peony. Rosa Picardy. Cowboy Jake. Blue-Sky Mother. Barnstable Father. Old Forty-Nine" (19)—"better than I do my parents" (21).

The first *real* memory of her parents that Morag feels she can trust to some degree—*"Although I can't trust it completely, either, partly because I recognize anomalies in it, ways of expressing the remembering, ways which aren't those of a five-year-old,"* she thinks (21)—is that of her mother's illness, the one that eventually kills her, thus linking the memory with a death scene: *"The whole thing was so quiet. No outer drama. That was the way, there"* (21). From this initial illness, the secret of her parents' demise begins for Morag, for she is not allowed to see her parents as their health declines. She cannot imagine the death scene, but she has a yearning for knowledge of it, and this lack of information increases the sense of loss Morag feels at their death.

When Morag first becomes aware of her parents' illness, she attempts to go upstairs to see them, but she is denied permission to make contact with them. Morag is confused about the events occurring around her, and she is unsettled by this lack of knowledge: "Something is happening. Morag senses it but cannot figure it out. Mrs. Pearl is trying to be kind. Morag is scared, and her stomach aches. If she eats anything, she will throw up" (22). Morag seeks comforting from her parents, and yearns for their protection in this moment of confusion: "I want to see my mother. . . . I am going up to see her right now. I won't stay long, Mrs. Pearl. I promise" (23). Yet social convention, presented in the form of Mrs. Pearl, "the Big Person," dictates that children not be allowed to see their parents when they are dying. Morag shows her awareness of this information when she promises not to stay long. Mrs. Pearl's response, however, while perhaps not intended to be mean-spirited, has that appearance to Morag: "They're too sick to see you, just now, Morag. They don't want to see you" (23).

The enforced absence of her parents becomes, with this pronouncement, a rejection of Morag, in her own young eyes, by her parents. Despite her protestation to the contrary— "You don't know anything about it! They do *so!* Let go of me!" (23)—the seeds of doubt have now been planted in her mind. Literary critic Marcienne Rocard aptly terms Morag a dispossessed figure, arguing that "Morag feels as if, through the loss of her physical parents, she has been deprived of a past."[14] Yet

Morag feels more than being deprived of parents and a past; she feels as though she has been ousted from her family: *her parents have dispossessed her.* This conclusion is reinforced in Morag by Mrs. Pearl's announcement that "they have passed on . . . to a happier land" (24).

The sense of a void or absence in the death scene is confirmed by the number of memories she has that refer to emptiness. Morag, locked in the kitchen, senses only silence from upstairs: "During the nights, there have been no sounds from upstairs" (24). On one occasion, Morag is able to escape the normally locked kitchen, but what she hears frightens her away from her exploration. Filling the void is a sound emanating from her father, but it is not a noise she attributes to humans: "From upstairs, there is a sound. Crying. Crying? Yes, crying. Not like people, though. Like something else. She does not know what. Kiy-oots. She knows only that it is her father's voice. There is no sound of her mother's voice, no sound at all" (24). The knowledge that Morag gains of her parents' illness is made doubly devastating with this cry, for, at first, there was the imposed void of the parents upstairs, out of reach of Morag, but what she now experiences is "terrifying," rather than comforting. Her father sounds like a coyote crying, so, when Morag finally has knowledge of her parents, it is information that scars her rather than helps her.

Later, when Morag is told of their deaths, she invokes her knowledge of death, which is limited to animals, to explain how they died: "She knows they are dead. She knows what dead means. She has seen dead gophers, run over by cars or shot, their guts redly squashed out on the road" (24). Morag is not allowed to see her parents in their deathbeds, despite her request, so she is not able to revise her vision of them as looking like the gophers: in the end, "Morag does not know how much of their guts lie coiled like scarlet snakes across the sheets" (24-5). She does not witness her parents' removal from the house; when she goes upstairs to look for them, "everybody has gone. Vanished" (25). She wonders, *"What was happening to everyone else? What really happened in the upstairs bedroom? No—the two bedrooms"* (22). Burning in Morag's mind is the question of what really happened. Morag becomes a victim here of the socially conditioned modes of dealing with death. Children were to be kept away from real experience of death, but the side effect was a wound created in Morag that gnaws at her throughout her life. Cognizance of her parents' death is something she can never retrieve or reconstruct.

The description of Morag's experience of her parents' death is presented almost as a contradiction of more contemporary approaches to dealing with children and death,[15] for she is kept in ignorance about the development and seriousness of her parents' illness, and she is deprived of the option of attending the funeral. While Mrs. Pearl encourages her to cry, there is really no opportunity for Morag to express her bewilderment. Christie and Prin may come to be loving foster parents, but Morag's new situation is so alien to her that it takes half a lifetime for her to realize the benevolence of her new parents. Counselling is a non-issue for Morag: she must learn her own independent ways of counselling herself; this is a task she is only now learning to do effectively. The end result of the treatment of Morag's grief is that she is confused by the events that occur in her life, and she feels a great sense of loss that is only explained by the vanishing of her parents.

In the present of the narrative, Morag asserts the elemental void at the heart of her memories of her parents: *"They remain shadows. Two sepia shadows on an old snapshot, two barely moving shadows in my head, shadows whose few remaining words and acts I have invented"* (27). The attempted writing of the death scene reinforces the absence of Morag's parents, but it also underscores Morag's essential and inevitable investment in her biological parents' existence, for "they're inside me," she thinks, *"flowing unknown in my blood and moving unrecognized in my skull"* (27). What she has to deal with in her lifetime is the irrecoverable fact of the absence. There is little consolation in the attempt at representing her parents fictionally, for it is fundamentally a failed attempt, as she has no referent for them. Out of this attempt at writing the death scene, however, comes the need to write a fiction of her life after the void, and that process allows the work of mourning to occur more effectively.

By contrast, in the second death scene that Morag figures, there is no lack of concrete images. In this scene Morag is brutally exposed to the horror of death, and specifically the physicality of death, in her experience of the fire at the Tonnerre shack in the Wachakwa Valley. Further, while emotionally very difficult for Morag, the experience of the corpses provides very concrete signifiers with which she can more fully understand the meaning of death. She later finds that signifying experience has tremendous narrative power when she tells Jules the story of the deaths, which ultimately helps him in his grieving and helps her in the writing of her text when she figures the deaths in her own narrative of mourning (the one we read).

When Lachlan MacLachlan, the editor of the *Manawaka Banner*, first assigns the story to Morag, his choice of words obscures what has happened in the fire, for he uses terms that only implicitly indicate the horror of the deaths by fire: "There's been a fire down in the valley, at the old Tonnerre shack, Morag. The older girl—what's her name?—and her two kids were caught in it. You better go down and see what's happened" (173). Morag at first does not understand Lachlan's meaning, and this, in part, perhaps, adds to the shock of her response when she arrives at the shack to research her story for the *Banner*: "For an instant Morag fails to understand what *caught in it* means. Then realizes" (173). Her first reaction is to shy away from the assignment, which is informed in part by a natural fear of what she might encounter, but also by her friendship with Jules and her acquaintance with Piquette. In this respect, this will be the most personal experience of loss, apart from her parents' deaths, that Morag has encountered in her life to date.

When Morag arrives at the Tonnerre shack, she notices "a sweetish nauseating odour" she cannot immediately identify. She also realizes the "smokened metal and burnt wood" of the shack is occupied by the burned corpses that she identifies, in her mind, by the bitterly ironic phrase "Burnt wood. *Bois Brûlés*" (175). When the corpses are brought out, Morag catches a glimpse of the bodies and "Vomits terribly into the snow" (175) in reaction to the horror of it. Later, when Morag has returned to the offices of the *Banner*, she is overcome by emotion: "Without warning, taking herself by surprise, she puts her head down on the desk and cries in a way she does not remember ever having done before, as though pain were the only condition in life" (176). The encounter with the burned corpses, of being directly exposed to the corporeality of death, has brought a new level of emotion and grief to Morag's experience.

Many years later, after her marriage with Brooke has deteriorated, Morag discovers she is the only living person in possession of knowledge of the scene of the burned shack. Morag is reluctant to pass on her knowledge, even to Jules—"I don't want to. I can't" (295)—but Jules needs to know what happened so he can mourn the deaths himself: "Tell me how my sister died. I have to know" (295). And Morag thinks, acknowledging the role her telling has in his grieving, "Why does he have to inflict this upon himself? Why can't he let it go? Perhaps he has to know before he can let it go at all" (296). The memory of the deaths is still so vivid in Morag's mind that an immediate physical reaction is elicited by Jules's request: "Morag gets up from the bed abruptly. Goes to the sink and vomits" (295), and then she tells him the one detail that will bring the horror of death so close to both their minds: the specific smell of burned corpse that is so very much out of the ordinary but that actually seems so banal. Morag tells him the air "smelled of—well, like roasted meat" (296). This realization by Morag is a chronicling of the qualities of human bodies, that they are, in fact, flesh and bone and will have the constitution of animal flesh.[16]

The story Morag tells Jules of the death of his sister and her children has no kinship with the World War II reports of death she read in the papers, nor with the poetic representations she has run across in her schooling.[17] Rather, it is a brutally honest and vivid representation that does not try in any way to obscure the realities of the deaths. The effect Morag's story has on Jules is that it frees him to mourn and memorialize his sister, which he does in the form of Piquette's Song, thus enabling him to figure deaths he has not experienced. He finds consolation in this act of representing a death experience once removed, but, ironically, Morag herself has no one to tell her the story of her parents' deaths. Thus, this experience of the death scene brings a new awareness of the importance of naming or articulating the corporeality of death, and the retelling in her text reinforces this significance.

The next death scene Morag writes depicts her return to Manawaka because Prin is dying. She is forced to look back on her departure from the town and to recognize she has made mistakes in her relationship with both Prin and Christie. This death scene clearly shows the destabilizing effect a death can have on the survivors, for Morag re-evaluates the life she is living; it is the news of the eventual death that forces her recognition that she has been living a false life with Brooke and that ignoring the past will not make the present more bearable.[18] Morag feels guilt at how she has conducted herself, and she is also brutally honest with herself about how she has treated her surrogate parents: "Had it been wrong to get away? No. Not wrong to want to get away, to make her get-away. It was the other thing that was wrong, the turning away, turning her back on the both of them. *The* both of them" (267). While Brooke played a heavy hand in causing Morag to turn away from her past, to deny it, Morag recognizes her own acquiescence in the act of avoidance. However, when she returns to Manawaka, she finds herself "thinking in the old phraseology" (268), the discourse of home. And so, when Morag goes back to Brooke, she no longer has the desire to repress her past, and the acknowledgement of that marks the beginning of the end of their relationship.

Effectively, Prin's death has caused Morag to re-evaluate her priorities, and the changes she makes—is compelled to make if she is to remain honest with herself—are directly born out of the death of her foster mother, the only mother she has ever known, and that, in itself, is an action of recognizing the importance and relation of Prin's life to her own:

> Since Prin's death, and the last sight of Christie, Morag has experienced increasingly the mad and potentially releasing desire to speak sometimes as Christie used to speak, the loony oratory, salt-beefed with oaths, the stringy lean oaths with some protein in them, the Protean oaths upon which she was reared. But of course does no such thing. (276)

However, the mere thought of the discourse offers the possibility of "release." Eventually, that is precisely what occurs, for Morag finally cannot continue her life as faculty-wife-cum-model-housewife, and she expresses herself in the discourse that is true to her upbringing, the words that are rooted in the parenting of Christie and Prin, whatever their shortcomings were. This is the voice of authenticity that now comes to her and speaks her desire for freedom from her oppressive life with Brooke:

"Brooke, I am twenty-eight years old, and I am five feet eight inches tall, which has always seemed too bloody christly tall to me but there it is, and by judas priest and all the sodden saints in fucking Beulah Land, I am stuck with it and I do not *mind* like I did once, in fact the goddam reverse if you really want to know, for I've gone against it long enough, and I'm no actress at heart, then, and that's the everlasting christly truth of it." (277)

From this outburst, Morag realizes that she has been suppressing her true voice all these years of being married to Brooke: "*I do not know the sound of my own voice. Not yet, anyhow*" (277).

The finding of her voice, however, is rooted in Morag's realization, throughout the process of Prin's dying and her funeral service, that she had turned her back on her upbringing, and that this was something she needed to acknowledge. Funeral rites, of course, are intended to move mourners through the liminal state brought on by the death, and for Morag these rites initiate a new liminal state for her—one that marks the end of her marriage. When Morag first arrives at the hospital, she encounters the medical discourse that only allows death when it is medically legitimized. Prin is, in all respects except the strictly physical, no longer alive, and there is nothing the hospital can do for her. However, Morag's pleas to the doctor for Prin's release from hospital, so she can die at home, are met with resistance: "I can't prevent you from discharging her against my advice, Mrs. Skelton," he says. "But she'd never stand the move" (269). But Morag is not convinced, and questions the medical opinion that seems callous and clinical, devoid of humanity and feeling for the patient: "'Why not? Why not?' But faced with this medical sanctity, Morag finds she cannot argue. And Christie's fighting days are over," she thinks (269). Finally, when Morag visits Prin's bedside: "At the first sight of Prin, Morag feels only relief that the doctor has had his way. Impossible, impossible to have Prin home. And then the reverse reaction. Who wouldn't prefer to die at home?" (269).

Prin appears, in her illness, already like a corpse—a living corpse. Her body lies "flaccid" and "quiet," and Morag thinks of her hair as the "wisps and straggling feathers of the almost-bald headskin, reminiscent (unbearably) of the dead half-bald baby birds fallen from nests in the spring of the year" (269). The face, too, is corpse-like to Morag, as she thinks, "Prin's face is as blank as a sheet of white paper upon which nothing will ever now be written. Her eyes are open and unseeing" (269-70). Prin is also unknowing, unable to recognize Morag, as the nurse is so quick to point out to her. When Prin dies a few days later, Morag reflects that Prin has been dead in spirit for many years, and now she is dead in body, too: "She has been in her sleep for years now, but whether there were dreams or nightmares in there, no one can know. Now at last there will be darkness" (270).[19]

Prin's funeral reflects Christie's description of Prin's life as "a bloody christly terrible life" (271). The funeral is held in the legitimized space of the church. As Morag notes, "Prin went to church for all those years, and liked the hymns, so it is only right and proper" (271), but the conditions of the funeral say much about the insignificance of Prin's life in the sphere of Manawaka society. The minister wonders, "Who will attend and sing?" (271) when Morag asks for a hymn to be added to the service for the dead, and a choir is out of the question because, as Morag infers, it is only possible if "the deceased is a well-known citizen" (272). Eleven people attend Prin's service, and the ones whom Morag recognizes are Eva Winkler, her new family, and her mother. The rest are what Morag terms "professional funeral attenders" (272). That the Winklers are the most prominent members of the congregation is instructive, for it is an accurate representation of Prin's place in Manawaka society.[20]

As Prin's death is revelatory of her life, so is Morag's experience of it. During the funeral service, Morag has an epiphanic moment. During the singing of the hymn "The Halls of Sion,"[21] she realizes that this vision of heaven is what she had expected of her life away from Manawaka and that what she has experienced, the life she has made with Brooke, is false: "Those halls of Sion. . . . The Prince is ever in them. What had Morag expected, those years ago, marrying Brooke? Those selfsame halls?" (273). Morag is humbled in her grief for Prin, and she realizes Prin has had a heretofore unacknowledged effect on Morag's life that Morag has tried very hard to forget over the years: "And now here, in this place, the woman who brought Morag up is lying dead" (274). The result is that Morag has a new-found sense of herself, and it is a harshly judged one: *"Help me, God; I'm frightened of myself"* (274). Fear has grown out of the acknowledgement that the erasure of the past, of her origins, has been a false strategy of living. Remaking herself as the housewife of a colonial English professor,[22] she realizes, has hidden her roots from herself— roots that, in the end, as she acknowledges through her experience of Prin's death, have shaped her identity as a woman, as a Canadian, and as a writer. Prin's life, laid bare in death (to its elemental core) is reflective of Morag's own life at this moment. The relations that matter most for Prin in death are familial—Christie and Morag. For Morag, too, then, recognition of the significance of familial ties becomes an elemental truth she can no longer elide. The inscription of Prin's death scene into the text Morag writes underscores its significance in the grand narrative of her life and denotes the importance of death rites and liminality as the means for moving on with life and for understanding ties to the deceased.

Christie's death, however, is the one that most disturbs Morag. It is the announcement of Christie's terminal illness that calls Morag back to Canada, a trip that results in her moving back permanently. Christie's illness and impending death are particularly disturbing for Morag because she comes to learn during her trip to Scotland that her reality—the frame of reference that matters the most to her—is rooted in the myths Christie recounted to her. Quite literally, her sense of reality is formed and shaped by the stories of Scotland, and the actual physical locations hold no meaning for her. Christie's "real country" (382) is what she affirms as her reality, a frame of reference that informs her general ontology.

When Morag returns to Manawaka, Dr. Cates tells her Christie is "not going to live forever" (416), and she is surprised by his mortality: "Isn't? And does this, obscurely and absurdly, come as a surprise?" she thinks (417). It is as if Christie has taken on larger-than-life proportions for Morag, perhaps in part because he has supplied her with a sense of history and myth, the elements that now give her a sense of reality and that frame her vision of the world and her place within it.

When Morag visits Christie in the hospital, the scene is clearly one of death. Christie is described as resembling a corpse, although he is still living: "He was never a large man, but now he seems to have shrunk even more. He appears to be composed of bones mainly, and of dried speckled brown skin, stretched over the skeleton" (418-19). The experience of medical treatment has altered the essential characteristics that marked Christie, as it did Prin, for "He is ludicrously clean-shaven, none of the greyish stubble on his face—they do that kind of thing for people in hospital" (419). The hospital has transformed Christie so that he no longer looks like himself: he has become sanitized in preparation for death. Hospitalization has subsumed Christie's dying into an institutional structure and procedure, depersonalizing the experience, as Morag finds out.

When the "tiny blonde nurse scurries in" and cheerily

announces "Bedpan time" (419), both Morag and Christie are disturbed, and their private moment of pain is shattered before they can connect:

> Christie's one good arm pushes weakly at the girl and the burden she bears. From his throat comes a sound which Morag has never before heard issuing from a human throat, and hopes never to hear again. A growl—the deep growl of a dog, combined with the wrenched-up sob of a man. (419-20)

The noise that emanates from Christie is similar to that heard from her father, linking the two at an elemental level of experience for Morag.[23] In this death scene the routine of the hospital takes away the dignity of the dying patient and his family. This scene is far removed from the stylized death scene so common to Victorian fiction, where the dignity of the dying person is paramount, but it is a harshly realistic vision of the difficulties of dying in "modern" society. Morag's outburst at the nurse's actions brings Christie out of his state of inertia—perhaps, in part, because he recognizes that Morag is displaying attributes of his own personality: "'For God's sake!' Morag cries. 'Can't you leave him be, just until I'm gone, then?'"; "'Get out,' Morag says fiercely. 'Just get out'" (420). Then, "When she looks at him, she is astonished. He has regained himself and is peering at her from his shroud of hospital linen, his eyes mocking and shrewd, his mouth in a soundless laugh" (420). Morag provides much-needed consolation for Christie when she tells him, "you've been my father to me" (420), and he can die with a positive sense of his relationship with Morag. By this "discovery" of the words she "must say" (420), Morag acknowledges the role Christie has had in her upbringing, and demonstrates that she has come to accept Christie as part of her ancestry.

Morag's initial reaction to Christie's death is one of extreme loneliness. She realizes that, with Christie dead, she is completely alone, without immediate family for support in the preparations for burial and mourning that are yet to come: "Now there is no one" (421). Morag remembers the grieving process when Prin died, where she was able to help Christie with his own bereavement, and he, too, contributed to her coping strategies: "When Prin died (a long time ago, it seems), Morag had to make all the funeral arrangements. Christie didn't do a thing. Still, he was there, and they held their wake for Prin, the two of them, sitting at the kitchen table with a bottle of whiskey between them" (421). Morag's first reactions to the tasks ahead of her are automatic: "Morag takes the necessary steps, robot steps, not thinking, not even thinking of mourning" (421).[24] Her response here is much more painful than it was to the other two deaths she has encountered, in part because she has come to realize over the years that Christie was, as she tells him on his deathbed, her father. This conclusion is supported by the fact that, after Prin's death, Morag reclaims the voice and discourse that is informed by Christie.

In making the preparations for Christie's burial, Morag's role is to mediate between his wishes for final burial and the options presented by a business that commodifies death,[25] and that is represented by a flashy man (Hector Jonas, who also appears in *A Jest of God*) with a "glittery plastic . . . veneer of himself" and a "public-relations act" (423). Morag feels that Christie should be buried in the Nuisance Grounds, now called the "Municipal Disposal Area,"[26] but she is met with incredulity by Hector, as he states, "Good Lord . . . you've got to be joking" (425). Morag is, of course, fully aware that this could not happen, as she explains her motives to Hector:

> "Yes, I know. Don't worry. It's all right. I know you can't
> just bury people anywhere, like that. It's just that—when
> Prin died, Christie said he'd like to have buried her in

the Nuisance Grounds. He didn't have much use for some things, although it's hard to explain." (425)

However, Morag negotiates her own changes to the common burial practices and bases them on what she thinks Christie would have wanted most.

Instead of cremation, which was Hector's suggestion—because "it's kind of the modern way" (426)—Morag wishes to have Christie buried beside his wife: "I want him buried in the Manawaka cemetery. . . . There is a small stone in that place for Prin. I want another one. Grey granite. With both their names" (426). Morag's most unusual request comes in the form of wanting a piper to signal Christie's burial. "Good Christ," says Hector, "A *what?*" (426). Morag wants only the piper, not "any service or talk," for she feels that this would be the most accurate tribute to Christie's life—a memorial that no other, more conventional, ritual could fulfill. Finally, she settles for a short service at the gravesite, if, ironically, "the minister will speak the words over Christie, who never went to church in his life" (426).

Christie's funeral, then, becomes a mediation between convention and Morag's attempt to stay true to the spirit of the man. In church, "there is no music, no oration, simply the bone-bare parts of the order of service, the old words," and the minister is anonymous; "Perhaps he even wonders who Christie was" (427), thinks Morag. It is only after the others have left, and Morag remains with Hector and the piper, that Christie can be memorialized properly by having the piper play "the long-ago pibroch, the lament for the dead, over Christie Logan's grave": "Morag sees, with the strength of conviction, that this is Christie's true burial" (428). And now Morag's thoughts enter into the realm of Christie's myth and legend: "*And Piper Gunn, he was a great tall man, with the voice of drums and the heart of a child, and the gall of a thousand, and the strength of conviction. . . .* And only now is Morag released into her mourning" (428). The funeral rites and the death properly attended become enormously beneficial for Morag's mourning.

The final death scene in *The Diviners* is an integral part of the framing text to the narrative that Morag writes, and it parallels the death scene of her parents, which is the first one she remembers. Morag becomes a consoling figure for Jules, as she helps him in his pain, and she has a mediating role in bringing Pique and Jules closer together. Where there was a void in her own experience in her parents' deaths, there is for Pique some presence, some knowledge of her father's death, and Morag becomes the bridging figure between the two.

Jules's death scene brings *The Diviners* to a close, for it has the function of enabling Pique and Morag to feel some sense of peace about Pique's departure west, and it also allows Morag the role of assisting Jules with his grief at his own impending death, for she consoles him in his moment of loss. Where the death scene of her parents is constructed as an entirely negative experience for Morag, Jules's is figured as a positive event—a death where the survivors are left, not with a void, but with something constructive with which to aid their mourning.

The parallels with the death scene of Morag's parents begin with Morag's invitation to visit Jules. Billy Joe, Jules's long-time friend and singing partner, calls Morag and asks her to come. While Jules has not asked Morag to come, the interchange between Billy Joe and Morag makes it clear that Jules would appreciate the visit.[27] Billy Joe's role in this scene is as facilitator to Jules's grief and to the needs of the survivors, unlike the role Mrs. Pearl fulfilled. Like her parents, Jules occupies rooms on the top floor of a house. Only here, "upstairs" is not a forbidden place, although it is an uncertain space until Morag enters it. Her five-year-old self never had the option of exploring the uncertain space to see for herself what was occurring within. When Billy Joe arrives outside Jules's room, he is uncertain about his actions, but driving his resolve is the sense that he is ultimately doing the right thing: "He looked oddly determined, as though he knew that this was necessary and what Jules wanted even though in an unadmitted way" (467).

Morag must now face the uncertainties, or unease, caused by the knowledge of experience. She knows that people on their deathbeds can be physically diminished, as Christie and Prin were:

> Now Morag was afraid. Not afraid, any longer, that Jules might mock her or tell her to get out. Not that, not now. Simply afraid of what she might see, of how he might look. Afraid that she might have to look at something she could not bear to look at. (467)

Her five-year-old self felt no self-consciousness about the need to visit her parents; it was simply expressed as desire, and, ultimately, as unfulfilled desire or need.

When Morag enters the room, she sees a Jules who is as he always has been: "He looked more like himself than the last time she had seen him. . . . His face looked bonier, but the same, the face of Skinner Tonnerre. . . . There were no outward signs of the sickness" (467-68). He does not appear wracked by illness, horribly contorted like Christie and Prin, nor is he incapable of communicating adequately, as they were. Morag asks herself, "What had she expected?" (468), but the question is answered by her experiences of past death scenes where the dying individual was a distorted vision of his or her previous self.

Rather than reacting in anger to Morag's appearance, he is accepting: "It's okay," he says. Morag's reaction to Jules is one of acceptance and of consolation. She knows there are many things she could do to help him, but she also has the sense that her very presence is what can have the most beneficial effect on him. As she thinks, "No way of talking to him any differently, now, than she ever had. No way of saying everything she would like to say, either. Maybe none of it needed saying, after all. . . . The thing now was not to interfere, not to enter fear" (468-69).

Unlike Christie and Prin, Jules dies at "home," away from the sanitized hospital deaths that are now the norm. He chooses to die on his own terms and in his own bed. In effect, he is able to die with dignity, rather than having it stripped away by institutions: "In the end, it would've made no damn difference. You think I want all that? People punching you here and there, tubes down your nose, parts of you cut like you were beef being butchered?" (469). It is then that Morag notices that Jules is "dwelling within the kind of physical pain which she never experienced and could not imagine" (469), and she gets the painkillers for him. Yet Morag, herself, becomes a consoling figure for Jules's psychic pain. She gives Jules the gift of his daughter's song, providing him with a sense of connection with her. While "his pain was lessened by the pills and the rye" (470), it is by reaching out to him physically—by simply being there to hold him—that Morag lessens the psychic pain somewhat:

> Finally Morag got up and turned out the light. Kicked off her shoes and lay down beside him, both of them clad, lying silently, connected only by their hands.
> Then Jules turned to her and put his arms around her, and she put her arms around him. (471)

The last sound she hears him utter parallels the final sound of her father Morag heard so many years ago, only now she is able to interpret what she hears from her accumulated knowledge of dying: "The brief sound in the darkness was the sound of a man crying the knowledge of his death" (471).

News of Jules's death comes four days later via Billy Joe, who does not embroider his death with a false story of a better place like Mrs. Pearl did. Rather, he simply says, "He's dead. . . . He didn't wait for it" (472). By relaying the means of death as suicide, Billy Joe articulates Jules's decision to define the terms of his death, and this decision differentiates Jules from each of the other dying figures in the novel.

In death, Jules now has dignity, for he is to be buried at Galloping Mountain: "The Métis graveyard up at the mountain, where the grey wooden crosses stood above the graves of the Tonnerres. Nearby, Jacques Tonnerre had his livingplace, his living place" (473). Morag has the role of communicating Jules's death to Pique, and, while Pique has not been allowed to see Jules before he died, she is given a sense of connection with him by the passing on of the knife, which is done through Morag. Unlike the young Morag, Pique has had experience, albeit not extensive, of her father, and she has something concrete upon which to base her search for identity. Morag wonders if Pique would "create a fiction out of Jules, something both more and less true than himself, when she finally made a song for him, as she would one day, the song he had never brought himself to make for himself?" (474). And in this lies the essential difference between Pique and Morag, for Morag had no knowledge of her parents and is not able to "create a fiction" out of them. She can only create a fiction out of the search for them, not out of knowing them.

The Diviners is Laurence's most complex and ambitious treatment of issues related to the work of mourning. In this final novel of the Manawaka series, Laurence was interested in exploring the relation between loss and writing. The roots of the creative drive are the focus of the book, for all Morag's creativity stems from the initial void created by her parents' deaths when she is five years old. When the novel opens, Morag's life has been rocked by Pique's departure. This crisis,

I have argued, is the catalyst for Morag's creative drive in the course of *The Diviners*. This drive leads her to revisit her past in the novel she writes. The fictional text she writes is a work of mourning, and my focus has been on the ordering principles of that text, for Morag figures the significant death scenes of her life and explores their significance in relation to her existence.

Laurence ends *The Diviners*, like *A Bird in the House*, on a positive note. Morag has completed the novel she has been composing over the course of the book, with only "the remaining private and fictional words" (477) left to compose. The closure implicit in the last lines of *The Diviners* reinforces the sense that Morag has moved out of the liminal state she occupied for most of the novel. The river is still "flowing both ways" (477), as in the opening sequence of the book, but Morag no longer sees an indeterminacy in the process of observing the flow. As her thoughts indicate, she has learned something about herself and her past by writing her novel. The past is seen as a repository of the shape of her future life, and she does not appear troubled by that notion: "*Look ahead into the past, and back into the future, until the silence*" (477).

AFTERWORD

LAURENCE AND
THE ELEGIAC TRADITION

In her five Manawaka novels, *The Stone Angel, A Jest of God, The Fire-Dwellers, A Bird in the House,* and *The Diviners,* Margaret Laurence explores the possibilities of the work of mourning. She places her protagonists in situations where they must come to terms with loss and where they must learn how to fashion their own ways of mourning. Laurence's examination of mourning most closely reflects the dual meanings of Freud's term *Trauerarbeit,* where the work of mourning as object—and as text—and as process is indicated. All her protagonists must learn how to mourn and then perform the labour of their mourning over the course of the novels. The first three protagonists struggle against socio-cultural and familial restrictions that censure the externalization of grief to carry out their work, and the final two employ the means of

writing to do that work. While all five mourn with great difficulty, they ultimately succeed at mourning and each book ends
with a moment of positive consolation.

It is this movement to a positive end to the grief work that
is significant in the Manawaka fiction, for Laurence demonstrates an adherence to psychoanalytic thinking that (following Freud) polarizes mourning and melancholia, indicating
that incomplete mourning is, in fact, a form of melancholia.
This fidelity is linked in large part to the strong intertext of
the pre-twentieth-century tradition of the English elegy,
where it is conventional to close the poem in a triumphant
moment of consolation. While the movement of mourning for
each protagonist reinforces the patterns of psychoanalytic
thinking and conventional elegy, Laurence ends each work by
subtly challenging the very notions of ideal mourning that she
patterns in her protagonists' psychic struggles.

The individual novels reflect paradigmatic similarities in
the way that the work of mourning is completed, but
Laurence also presents a spectrum of mourning women in the
Manawaka fiction where each protagonist reflects a significant
and different grieving situation. Hagar is depicted as being at
the end of her long life, accepting her own weakening body
but not able to mourn her impending death, and in a situation
where she has yet to effectively mourn the deaths of her husband Bram and her youngest son John. Rachel and Stacey, in
the sister novels, reflect the difficulties of mourning in the
mid- to late twentieth century most closely, for they encounter
a world that provides them with no meaningful structures
within which they can perform their labour of mourning.
Rachel is most obviously an individual in protracted, unresolved grief when the novel opens, and it is only through great
difficulty that she is able to fashion her own means of labouring at grief; Stacey, by contrast, mourns the state of the world
and finds herself unable to cope with living in a society

without clearly defined structures of meaning. She, too, must provide her own ways of coping.

Laurence's last two protagonists, Vanessa and Morag, are directly involved with issues related to the expression of grief, and the process of working through mourning, by writing a creative narrative. *A Bird in the House* is best seen as a book where Laurence explores the possibilities of the structuring qualities of narrative in relation to the organization of the work of mourning, for Vanessa is shown to learn about her own grief (while she performs her own labour of mourning) though the mourning experiences of other family members that she remembers and then writes into her stories, which are the stories we read. In the final novel of her writing career, Laurence most fully examines the ideas raised in *A Bird in the House*, for she identifies her protagonist as a novelist, a mourning individual, and as someone who is compelled to write her way through her grief. The term *thanatosroman* describes *The Diviners*, for Morag learns about grief, and how to grieve, by examining and structuring her novel through the figuring of death scenes. The *thanatosroman* is similar to the *kunstlerroman*, which is itself a subgenre of the *bildungsroman*, whereby the development of a life is explored. *The Diviners*, as a *thanatosroman*, borrows from both genres by examining the development of the novelist/artist figure in relation to the development of knowledge about death and grieving, while the novelist simultaneously works through deep feelings of loss associated with the deaths of her parents when she was a child by writing the text that we read.

The conclusion of the work of mourning for each protagonist—and even the fact that mourning is concluded—reflects the ideal of how mourning functions. The protagonists are all transformed in positive ways and thus Freud's notion of effective mourning, or normal mourning, is closely reflected in Laurence's novels. The pattern of the expression of emotions in Laurence's writing reinforces a psychoanalytic perspective even while her characters are shown to struggle, and then overcome, socio-cultural and familial constraints that limit emotional articulation. Grief is something to be laboured at and then worked through, and ultimately it is left behind. Jahan Ramazani notes that "Most clinical psychoanalysis has adapted normal, 'healthy,' or 'successful' mourning as a therapeutic ideal,"[1] and Kathleen Woodward states that "in psychoanalysis . . . the emotions are something to be eliminated, to be unearthed and discharged, to be gotten rid of, not something to be cultivated"; and "For Freud the most important aspect of this work of mourning is that it must come to an end."[2]

Laurence's adherence to the concept of the labour of mourning as a finite process, ending with a fully consoled mourner, is rooted in the processes of mourning figured in conventional English elegy. Laurence is not alone with her attention to matters of death and mourning in twentieth-century literature, of course, and she is easily placed alongside a tradition of fiction writers who figure mourning subjects, such as D.H. Lawrence, Thomas Mann, Alice Munro, Joy Kogawa, and Graham Swift, among many others. And while she does fit into such a paradigm, Laurence's consistent figuring of the positive ends of the work of mourning in these books underscores the strong intertext with conventional English poetic elegy that predates her own century.

John Milton's elegy "Lycidas" is a foundational poem in the English tradition, building on ancient elegies by Theocritus, Bion, Moschus, and Virgil, as well as on poems by the Renaissance English writers who precede him, Sidney and Spenser. The notion of a tradition of writing loss that reaches back thousands of years and that writers adapt in response to both their own immediate grieving needs as well as to the requirements of socio-cultural context is important to consider in relation to Laurence's work, for she, too, gestures to a heritage of elegy in her novels. Milton was acutely aware of the writers who preceded his engagement with mourning, but he also adapted earlier forms in response to his own immediate grieving as well as to the requirements of his own social context. "Lycidas" quickly became a point of reference—a key intertext—for later elegists such as Shelley in "Adonais" and Arnold in "Thyrsis," who carried on the pastoral mode as well as the deliberate dramatization of the labour of mourning evident in Milton's poem. It is this latter point, in particular, that is interesting for understanding Laurence's connection to the English tradition of elegy, for all three poems describe a movement of mourning that dramatically figures an elegist working through his grief, and this movement is akin to that of Laurence's protagonists. The work of mourning in these poems, and also in the Manawaka novels, is an occasion for labouring at grief, and, in Laurence's case, the occasion takes place over several weeks and months. For Milton's elegist, the dramatic action of the poem takes place over the course of a day as he sings his song of grief; for Arnold, the elegist takes a twilight walk through the countryside he used to roam with his lost friend Thyrsis. As Milton adapts the consolatory movement of his poem to allow for an apotheosis of the lost person to a Christian heaven, so, too, do Shelley and Arnold modify Milton's Christian perspective. Shelley's apotheosis occurs within a Neoplatonic vision of the world, and Arnold's afterlife is a return to an idealized pastoral world.

The opening lines of Milton's "Lycidas" reflect several key conventions of the genre that remain integral and are seen in Laurence's intertextual gestures towards the tradition:

> Yet once more, O ye laurels, and once more
> Ye myrtles brown, with ivy never sere,
> I come to pluck your berries harsh and crude,

And with forced fingers rude,
Shatter your leaves before the mellowing year.
Bitter constraint, and sad occasion dear,
Compels me to disturb your season due.

In the opening phrase, the elegist invokes the repetitive nature of elegy, that the process or mourning entered into by the composition of the poem is one that has occurred before and will, presumably, occur again. Milton asserts that experiences of loss and the labour of mourning that accompanies them are serial aspects of human existence. The next lines refer to the forced nature of entering into a work of mourning: loss is not predictable, and the ones left to mourn are "forced" to cope. The language of these passages reinforces the negative drama of being compelled to mourn—"rude," "Shatter," and "Bitter"—and the premature plucking of the leaves of poetic inspiration[3] underscores that all death is effectively too early for those left to mourn.

In the most fundamental of ways, Laurence repeatedly engages in the act of writing grief as she composes her five novels, of performing the labour of mourning, of returning over and over again to the key issues relating to loss and how to cope with the deaths of loved ones. She is like Milton's elegist, as each novel begins, who "Yet once more" is compelled to perform grief work. Milton is also an important touchstone for Laurence, as his elegist grieves with great success, as do all her protagonists. His poem ends with a movement of deep consolation where Lycidas transcends the physical living world in a triumphant apotheosis so that he is "sunk low" in physical death[4] "but mounted high" in heaven. As much as Laurence's characters struggle to articulate their work of mourning, they all come to a moment of anagnorisis and reversal by labouring over their grief.

Elegists for several centuries after Milton found his pattern of the successful work of mourning to be a convincing and useful model, for writers such as Dryden, Wordsworth, Shelley, and Tennyson also adopt a fundamentally positive stance towards the outcome of mourning. By the middle of the nineteenth century, however, Arnold begins to demonstrate a scepticism in the consolatory powers of elegy in "Dover Beach," and Thomas Hardy, in his turn-of-the-century poem "The Darkling Thrush," most fully expresses altering perspectives on the possibilities of completing a consolatory work of mourning; consolation in the elegy is undercut by the negativity of its expression. The voice of the "aged thrush, frail, gaunt, and small" who sings at the end of the day provides nothing positive for the elegist:

> So little cause for carolings
>   Of such ecstatic sound
> Was written on terrestrial things
>   Afar or nigh around,
> That I could think there trembled through
>   His happy good-night air
> Some blessed Hope, whereof he knew
>   And I was unaware.

This scepticism becomes key to elegiac practice in the twentieth century, in poetry and in fiction, so the notion of the fairly easily achieved consolation evaporates as a possibility. Jahan Ramazani remarks that "modern poets reanimate the elegy not by slavishly adopting its conventions; instead, they violate its norms and transgress its limits. They conjoin the elegiac with the anti-elegiac, at once appropriating and resisting the traditional psychology, structure, and imagery of the genre."[5] Further, "preeminent among their targets is the psychological propensity of the genre to translate grief into consolation."[6] But Laurence does not overtly challenge the compensatory nature of the labour of mourning, as do so many twentieth-century writers, aligning herself instead with the Miltonic tradition of elegy.

Laurence engages with the English tradition of elegy in other ways, too, for she repeatedly figures elements relating to death throughout the Manawaka series. In *The Stone Angel*, she opens the novel in a graveyard and pays close attention to the stone angel of the title—a grave marker—as well as other graves, in a strong allusion to Gray's "Elegy Written in a Country Church-Yard." The more general contemplation of life and death evident in Gray's poem is influential in other ways, as well. *A Jest of God* is rife with elements relating to death, for Rachel's father was an undertaker and she and her mother live above the funeral home. The novel presents a strong subtext that comments on the rapidly changing nature of the funeral business in the twentieth century. *The Fire-Dwellers* depicts a world that is itself apocalyptic. This is reinforced early in the novel when Stacey encounters the cenotaph in Vancouver that has lost its memorializing function within the ashen and fallen city she encounters.[7] Likewise, *A Bird in the House* and *The Diviners* are rife with images of death, funerals, and graveyards. Vanessa remembers several funerals over the course of the book. Similarly, Morag in the final novel considers the graves of her parents in the cemetery in addition to writing several funerals into her text.

The ambiguous endings of the final four novels (*The Stone Angel*, of course, ends with Hagar's final thoughts as she dies and thus would not fit the pattern) indicate that Laurence is not fully convinced that the emotions should be discharged and left behind, however. *A Jest of God* and *The Fire-Dwellers* are exemplary of Laurence's position. Rachel's story ends with her acceptance of the uncertainty of life but it is clear that the work of mourning has been completed. She is more willing than before to accept that emotions must be articulated when necessary and she acknowledges she may have to return to re-examine old losses when needed: "I do not know how many bones need be broken before I can walk" (208). At the end of the novel she acknowledges she has learned how to labour at mourning and that this knowledge may serve her in the future. Indeed, the whole final section of *A Jest of God* reflects Rachel's acceptance of uncertainty, that things can and will change. As she thinks of her future self: "I will be afraid. Sometimes I will feel lighthearted, sometimes light-headed. I may sing aloud, even in the dark. I will ask myself if I am going mad, but if I do, I won't know it" (209). Stacey's story of inner turmoil ends with her falling asleep and the troubles of life she has been facing are in the background rather than the foreground of her consciousness, but the question that ends the novel indicates that Laurence is uneasy about such a conclusive termination and that she prefers instead the possibility that all that Stacey has gone through may well return again: "[Stacey] feels the city receding as she slides into sleep. Will it return tomorrow?" Thus, the work of mourning for Stacey may be circular or cyclical, rather than final. This not quite the cultivation of emotion that Woodward describes, but is an acknowledgment that psychic trauma such as grief is not easily—or perhaps ever—put aside.

Of the final two novels, *A Bird in the House* ends most clearly with the conclusion of the process of mourning. In the last paragraphs of the book, Vanessa uses the clinical language of mourning to describe her grief for her mother, invoking the discourse of disease so common to psychoanalytic parlance: "Of all the deaths in the family, hers remained unhealed in my mind longest" (190). And when she leaves Manawaka, the finality of her words—"I sensed that this would be my last sight of it" (190)—reinforces the notion that her grief is laid to rest and the wound of loss will not be revisited. The ending of *The Diviners*, however, is subtly ambiguous, similar to the sister novels. The river that serves as a metaphor for the paradoxical process of looking to the past to deal with the future in the opening passages of the novel is returned to here. By the process of working through grief by writing a novel of her mourning, Morag has perhaps gained knowledge of the losses she suffers, but she also acknowledges the process was not all-revealing. The work of mourning can only do so much, and it will possibly have to be undertaken again:

> How far could anyone see into the river? Not far. Near the shore, in the shallows, the water was clear, and there were clean and broken clamshells of creatures now dead, and the wavering underwater weed-forest, and the flicker of small live fishes, and the undulating lines of gold as the sand ripples received the sun. Only slightly further out, the water deepened and kept its life hidden from sight. (477)

I want to end by considering Arthur W. Frank's words, in *The Wounded Storyteller: Body, Illness, and Ethics*, where he considers the notion of writing out of suffering:

> The figure of the storyteller is ancient: Tiresias, the seer who reveals to Oedipus the true story of whose son he is, has been blinded by the gods. His wound gives him his narrative power. The wound that the biblical patriarch Jacob suffers to his hip while wrestling with an angel is part of the story he tells of that event, and it is the price of his story. As he tells his story to those he returns to— and who else could have told it?—his wound is evidence of his story's truth.[8]

Margaret Laurence, in the Manawaka fiction, is similar to the elegist of any age, for the wounds she writes of are the psychic wounds of loss, and the works of mourning that are the result of the labour of grief are the evidence of the depth of loss she experienced. Hagar in *The Stone Angel*, Rachel in *A Jest of God*, and Stacey in *The Fire-Dwellers* reflect Laurence's exploration of the difficulties of grappling with loss and of struggling to articulate that loss. Laurence's two writer narrators, Morag in

The Diviners and Vanessa in *A Bird in the House*, reflect her examination of how loss can provide power to narrate, as with Tiresias, so that the stories of grief from the past can be told. Morag's and Vanessa's stories and Laurence's Manawaka fiction are, paradoxically, about the losses that impel the storytelling itself, and so, like Jacob, the price of the story is the content. This pain of loss and storytelling is characteristic of the Manawaka fiction and bears witness to the struggle of the labour of grief, of the work of mourning.

ENDNOTES

INTRODUCTION

1. I follow Thomas Attig, who states, in *How We Grieve: Relearning the World* (New York: Oxford University Press, 1996), that "writings on grieving and mourning define the terms variously and sometimes ambiguously. Without an extensive defense of my choices, I intend to use the terms *grieving* and *mourning* to refer to processes accommodating to loss" (8).

2. The Middle Ages are well served by examples from anonymous authors: works such as *Beowulf*, the *Song of Roland*, or *Morte Arthure*, are representative.

3. The town of Manawaka is a fictional rendition of her hometown, Neepawa, Manitoba.

4. For an important study of grief in Munro and Gallant, see Karen E. Smythe, *Figuring Grief: Gallant, Munro, and the Poetics of Elegy* (Montreal and Kingston: McGill-Queen's University Press, 1992). Recent Canadian writing has explored this area of cultural expression, although criticism, with the exception of Smythe's work, has not followed suit. Other useful and interesting examples of explorations of mourning can be found in *Badlands* by Kroetsch, *In a Glass House* by Ricci, *Obasan* by Kogawa, and *Disappearing Moon Café* by Lee, for example. It is also worth noting that Laurence's elegiac legacy is evident in the work of two key contemporary prairie writers, Kristjana Gunnars and Aritha van Herk, who further develop Laurence's interest in death and grief.

5. James King, *The Life of Margaret Laurence* (Toronto: Knopf, 1997), 25.

6. Ibid., 25.

7. Margaret Laurence, *Dance on the Earth: A Memoir* (Toronto: McClelland and Stewart, 1989), 25.

8. Ibid., 25.

9. Though seemingly a minor point, it is worth noting that Laurence subtly reinforces the related nature of her protagonists. Rachel, in *A Jest of God*, and Stacey, in *The Fire-Dwellers*, are sisters, and Stacey, Vanessa, from *A Bird in the House*, and Morag, from *The Diviners*, are all classmates at school. Quotations from the

Manawaka books are taken from the following editions: *The Stone Angel*, NCL (Toronto: McClelland and Stewart, 1964); *A Jest of God*, NCL (Toronto: McClelland and Stewart, 1966); *The Fire-Dwellers*, NCL (Toronto: McClelland and Stewart, 1969); *A Bird in the House*, NCL (Toronto: McClelland and Stewart, 1970); and *The Diviners*, NCL (Toronto: McClelland and Stewart, 1974).

10. James King, in *The Life of Margaret Laurence*, notes that Laurence's losses "were difficult for her to come to terms with except in writing" (163).

11. Peter Marris, *Loss and Change* (Garden City: Anchor Press/ Doubleday, 1975), 26.

12. Jacques Derrida, *The Work of Mourning*, ed. Pascale-Anne Breault and Michael Naas (Chicago and London: University of Chicago Press, 2001), 95.

13. David Mellor, "Death in High Modernity: The Contemporary Presence and Absence of Death," in *The Sociology of Death: Theory, Culture, Practice*, ed. David Clark (Oxford: Blackwell/*The Sociological Review*, 1993), 12. Ontological security, as Mellor quotes social theorist Anthony Giddens, refers to an individual's "sense of order and continuity in relation to the events in which they participate, and the experiences they have, in their day-to-day lives," 12.

14. Ibid., 13.

15. Ester R. Shapiro, *Grief as a Family Process: A Developmental Approach to Clinical Practice* (New York and London: The Guilford Press, 1994), 4.

16. I would like to thank James King for signalling to me the importance of Bowlby's revision of Freud. John Bowlby, *Loss: Sadness and Depression* (London: Pimlico, 1980), 17. While variously constituted in the specific processes involved, the general notion of the gradual breaking of the emotional connection to the dead person in order to move on is a common and accepted one in psychological writing. Formal theorization begins with Freud in his essay "Mourning and Melancholia" (1917), but includes numerous commentators. Among these are David A. Crenshaw in *Bereavement: Counseling the Grieving Throughout the Life Cycle* (New York: Continuum, 1990), Peter Marris in *Loss and Change*, Beverly Raphael in *The Anatomy of Bereavement* (New York: Basic

Books, 1983), and Elizabeth Kübler-Ross in *On Death and Dying* (London: Macmillan, 1969).

17. See Sigmund Freud, "Mourning and Melancholia," in *A General Selection From the Works of Sigmund Freud*, ed. John Rickman (Garden City: Doubleday, 1957), 124-40.

18. In the words of Neal Tolchin, "an unresolved experience of bereavement . . . can lie dormant and revive periodically throughout one's life." Neal Tolchin, *Mourning, Gender, and Creativity in the Art of Herman Melville* (New Haven and London: Yale University Press, 1993), 5. Tolchin points out that, "because it is such a new field, thanatology has yet to produce the studies needed to analyze the tenuous line between normal and pathological mourning." See *Mourning, Gender, and Creativity*, 6.

19. Tolchin, *Mourning, Gender, and Creativity*, 5.

20. Freud, "Mourning and Melancholia," 126. Later on the same page he refers to "mental economics," reinforcing this image of labour and complexity.

21. Freud states: "The task [of mourning] is . . . carried through bit by bit, under great expense of time and cathectic energy." See Freud, "Mourning and Melancholia," 126.

22. Robert Kastenbaum, *Death, Society and Human Experience* (Boston: Allyn and Bacon, 1995), 321-22. Literary critic and theorist Kathleen Woodward provides a useful delineation of Freud's definition of mourning:

> [Mourning] is psychic work which has a precise purpose and goal—to "free" ourselves from the emotional bonds which have tied us to the person we loved so that we may "invest" that energy elsewhere, to "detach" ourselves so that we may be "uninhibited." Mourning is "necessary." It denotes a process which takes place over a long period of time. It is slow, infinitessimaly so, as we simultaneously psychically cling to what has been lost.

See "Late Theory, Late Style: Loss and Renewal in Freud and Barthes," in *Aging and Gender in Literature: Studies in Creativity*, ed. Anne M. Wyatt-Brown and Janice Rosen (Charlottesville and London: University Press of Virginia, 1993), 85.

23. Richard Stamelman, *Lost Beyond Telling: Representations of Death*

and Absence in Modern French Poetry (Ithaca and London: Cornell University Press, 1990), 50-51.

24. Derrida, *The Work of Mourning*, 142. These words are from a talk Derrida gave at a conference honouring Louis Marin. Derrida's words serve in themselves as a self-conscious work of mourning, while at the same time further defining the concept. Derrida discusses the "image," meaning here a visual image, as in a created image (such as a visual artist would produce), but primarily he means the image of the dead person. In a piece written after the death of Gilles Deleuze, he attempts to describe the image of Deleuze in death, calling it an "unimaginable image." See *The Work of Mourning*, 192.

25. Ibid., 142.

26. Stamelman, *Lost Beyond Telling*, 19.

27. John J. Clayton, *Gestures of Healing: Anxiety and the Modern Novel* (Amherst: The University of Massachusetts Press, 1991), 4.

28. Margaret Laurence, "Time and the Narrative Voice," in *A Place to Stand On: Essays by and about Margaret Laurence*, ed. George Woodcock (Edmonton: NeWest Press, 1983), 155.

29. As Bowlby states, "an occasional recurrence of active grieving, especially when some event reminds the bereaved of her loss, is the rule." See *Loss*, 101.

30. Tolchin, *Mourning, Gender, and Creativity*, 167.

31. See Victor Turner, *Dramas, Fields, and Metaphors: Symbolic Action in Human Society* (New Ithaca and London: Cornell University Press, 1974); "Variations on a Theme of Liminality," in *Secular Ritual*, ed. S.F. Moore and B.G. Meyerhoff (Amsterdam: Van Gorcum, 1977); and *The Anthropology of Performance* (New York: PAJ Publications, 1986).

32. Arnold van Gennep, *The Rites of Passage*, trans. Monika B. Vizedom and Gabrielle L. Caffee (Chicago: The University of Chicago Press, 1960), 11.

33. Van Gennep argues: "a complete scheme of rites of passage theoretically includes preliminal rites (rites of separation), liminal rites (rites of transition), and postliminal rites (rites of incorporation)." See *The Rites of Passage*, 11.

34. Jill G. Morawski, *Practising Feminisms, Reconstructing Psychology:*

Notes on a Liminal Science (Ann Arbor: The University of Michigan Press, 1994), 54.

35. Turner, "Variations on a Theme of Liminality," 37.

36. Literary critic Gustavo Prez Firmat argues that "liminality should be looked upon not only as a transition between states but as a state in itself." See *Literature and Liminality: Festive Readings in the Hispanic Tradition* (Durham: Duke University Press, 1986), 20.

37. The exceptions are when memories of the immediate reactions to death resurface in Laurence's protagonists. Hagar, for example, remembers being numbed by John's death, and Morag describes herself as an automaton after Christie dies.

38. Clinical psychologist Beverly Raphael notes that phases of mourning "are not clear-cut or fixed, and that the bereaved may pass backward and forward among them." See *The Anatomy of Bereavement* (New York: Basic Books, 1983), 33-34. Another clinical psychologist, Therese A. Rando, remarks, "the speed of the progress is not important as long as progress is being made," reinforcing the long passage of time that Laurence depicts for the mourning of her protagonists. See *Grief, Dying, and Death: Clinical Interventions for Caregivers* (Champaign, Ill: Research Press, 1984), 28.

39. Tolchin, *Mourning, Gender, and Creativity*, 167.

40. Bowlby, *Loss*, 94.

41. Ibid.

42. Thomas Attig, *How We Grieve*, 116.

CHAPTER ONE

1. Jon Kertzer, "*The Stone Angel*: Time and Responsibility," *The Dalhousie Review* 54, 3 (1972): 500. Brenda Beckman-Long, in "*The Stone Angel* as a Feminine Confessional Novel," in *Challenging Territory: The Writing of Margaret Laurence*, ed. Christian Riegel (Edmonton: University of Alberta Press, 1997), 47, makes a similar point when she states that "[Hagar's] narrative is an attempt to unify memories of the past and experiences of the present in one account, and it culminates in the attainment of insight into herself"; and Shirley Chew, in "'Some Truer Image':

A Reading of *The Stone Angel*," in *Critical Approaches to the Fiction of Margaret Laurence*, ed. Colin Nicholson (Vancouver: University of British Columbia Press, 1990), 37, remarks that "events of the past are recovered from a point further on in time, and with the understanding which hindsight affords." In "Hagar's Old Age: *The Stone Angel as Vollendungsroman*," in *Crossing the River: Essays in Honour of Margaret Laurence*, ed. Kristjana Gunnars (Winnipeg: Turnstone Press, 1988), 31, Constance Rooke terms the novel a "*Vollendungsroman*," which is "the novel of 'completion' or 'winding down'," and David Williams, in *Confessional Fictions: A Portrait of the Artist in the Canadian Novel* (Toronto: University of Toronto Press, 1991), 86, specifies that *The Stone Angel* is about Hagar's "meditation on approaching death. . . . Hagar's story . . . is a monumental pose, told to *herself* to free her from the threat of nature," 86.

2. I group the gravestone of her mother and the death scenes together here because Hagar did not, of course, witness or have direct knowledge of her mother's death. The closest she can come to figuring her mother's death is by describing the stone angel.

3. King, *The Life of Margaret Laurence*, 161.

4. Michel Fabré, "The Angel and Living Water: Metaphorical Networks and Structural Opposition in *The Stone Angel*," in *New Perspectives on Margaret Laurence: Poetic Narrative, Multiculturalism, and Feminism*, ed. Greta Coger (Westport and London: Greenwood Press, 1996), 18.

5. Alice Bell, "Hagar Shipley's Rage for Life: Narrative Technique in *The Stone Angel*," in *New Perspectives on Margaret Laurence: Poetic Narrative, Multiculturalism, and Feminism*, ed. Greta Coger (Westport and London: Greenwood Press, 1996), 51.

6. Simone Vauthier also notes that the stone angel "is also her father's monument, a symbol of his attitude towards his family, the community and life." See "Images in Stones, Images in Words: Margaret Laurence's *The Stone Angel*," in *Critical Approaches to the Fiction of Margaret Laurence*, ed. Colin Nicholson (Vancouver: University of British Columbia Press, 1990), 50.

7. After all these years, Hagar still remembers the inscription: "*Rest in peace. / From toil, surcease. / Regina Weese. /1886*" (4).

8. Laurence alludes to the conventions of elegy, and specifically pastoral elegy, in these passages in the Manawaka graveyard. The

"thistles," "cowslips"—"wild and gaudy flowers"—grow along-side the "portly peonies" (5), reflecting John Milton's laurels, myrtles, and ivy, with their "berries harsh and crude" in his foundational pastoral elegy "Lycidas." The "scrub oak" (5) in the same passage in the novel echoes Thomas Gray's "Elegy Written in a Country Church-Yard" with its "rugged elms" that overlook the gravestones.

9. While Hagar becomes dependent upon Bram by marrying him, the departure from home is a statement of her independence from her father, in her eyes. She feels she is taking a stand about her life, and she revels in keeping house for Bram, despite its being an alien occupation for her. It is only later that she finds life with him confining and limiting.

10. The rest of the passage continues the apology: "I wouldn't want you to feel you always had to be going out somewhere. You could come here in the evenings. I wouldn't say a word. I could go into the front room, or upstairs, if you liked. I'd not get in your way. Wouldn't that be a good idea?" (247).

CHAPTER TWO

1. Theo Quayle Dombrowski, "Word and Fact: Laurence and Language," *Canadian Literature*, 80 (1979): 51; Helen M. Buss, *Mother and Daughter Relationships in the Manawaka Works of Margaret Laurence* (Victoria: University of Victoria, 1985), 32; Aritha van Herk, "The Eulalias of Spinsters and Undertakers," in *Crossing the River: Essays in Honour of Margaret Laurence*, ed. Kristjana Gunnars (Winnipeg: Turnstone Press, 1988), 136.

2. My focus is on how death contributes to Rachel's constriction. Nora Stovel provides an insightful and thorough examination of how "Rachel's real enemy . . . is the town, for Manawaka imprisons Rachel with manacles of repression that stifle her freedom." See Nora Stovel, *Rachel's Children: Margaret Laurence's 'A Jest of God'* (Toronto: ECW Press, 1992), 27-32 and passim. Stovel's work has been particularly useful to me here as she carefully delineates the pervasive nature of death-related matters in Rachel's consciousness and life and also in Manawaka itself.

3. Jill Franks, "Jesting Within: Voices of Irony and Parody as Expressions of Feminisms," in *Challenging Territory: The Writing of*

Margaret Laurence, ed. Christian Riegel (Edmonton: University of Alberta Press, 1997), 104.

4. King, *The Life of Margaret Laurence*, 229.

5. Philip Ariès, *The Hour of Our Death*, trans. Helen Weaver (New York: Knopf, 1981), 580.

6. Geoffrey Gorer, *Death, Grief and Mourning in Contemporary Britain* (Garden City, NJ: Doubleday, 1965), 18, 20. Although Gorer is writing specifically about the middle of this century— close to Rachel's own time—his comments seem still to be applicable to society's general reaction to the physical realities of death. Sociologist Glennys Howarth comments on the difficulties involved in studying mortuary practices. She notes that no funeral home was willing to show her the "secret" back rooms where bodies are prepared for burial. See Glennys Howarth, "Investigating Deathwork: a personal account," in *The Sociology of Death: Theory, Culture, Practice*, ed. David Clark (Oxford: Blackwell/*The Sociological Review*, 1993), 221-38.

7. Philip Ariès, *Western Attitudes Towards Death: From the Middle Ages to the Present*, trans. Patricia M. Ranum (Baltimore and London: Johns Hopkins University Press, 1974), 87.

8. Ariès, *The Hour*, 580.

9. In *The Anatomy of Bereavement*, psychologist Beverly Raphael remarks:

> Dread of the dead body, the dead person, appears in most societies and cultures. Special rituals have been evolved to deal with it and to separate it from the living. These rituals may have a medical and scientific framework as in Western society. . . . The medicalization of death in contemporary Western society seems to have carried this ritualization to extremes. The dead are mysteriously whisked away to the mortuary, ice cold, clinical, and impersonal. Most medical institutions provide little opportunity or even a place where the bereaved can be with the dead person in privacy and closeness for last farewells (36-37).

While corpses are still taboo in western societies, bodies themselves are re-entering the public sphere, as evidenced by the proliferation of television programs featuring graphic surgery and real emergency-room scenarios.

10. Mikhail M. Bakhtin, *Problems of Dostoevsky's Poetics*, trans. and ed. Caryl Emerson (Minneapolis: University of Minnesota Press, 1984), 195.

11. William McClellan, "The Dialogic Other: Bakhtin's Theory of Rhetoric," *Bakhtin and Otherness. Discours Social / Social Discourse: International Research Papers in Comparative Literature*, 3, 1 & 2 (1990), ed. Robert F. Barsky and Michael Holquist, 233.

12. Doubleness is reinforced by Rachel's punning, where her words provide play reinforcing the slippage she feels as she sits "rapt" and "wrapped."

13. Ariès, *The Hour*, 580.

14. van Herk, "The Eulalias of Spinsters," 139. Other literary critics, too, have remarked upon the importance of Rachel's sexual experiences in the novel. Nancy Bailey, in "Psychology of Re-birth in *A Jest of God*," *Journal of Popular Culture* 15 (1981): 62, notes Rachel's "problems of repressed sexuality," Helen Buss, in *Mother and Daughter Relationships*, states that her growth is "aided by her sexual relationship with Nick" (40), and Mathew Martin, in "Dramas of Desire in Margaret Laurence's *A Jest of God, The Fire-Dwellers*, and *The Diviners*," *Studies in Canadian Literature* 22, no. 1 (1995): 58-9, indicates that "Rachel reworks the structure of her desire in the personal sphere" by moving away from the Oedipal fixation on her father to a focus on her own fulfillment. In "That Fool of a Fear: Notes on *A Jest of God*," in *A Place to Stand On: Essays by and about Margaret Laurence*, ed. George Woodcock (Edmonton: NeWest Press, 1983), 218, George Bowering confirms these interpretations by stating that "I see the change in Rachel's consciousness as a result of her getting in touch with her body, that part the Scottish Christians preferred to cover with rough wool and to forget."

15. Bowlby, *Loss*, 23.

16. Stovel, *Rachel's Children*, 47.

17. Running through Rachel's head are thoughts of Edgar Allan Poe, involving ideas of gothic horror, as well as her ironic sense of humour: "My fingers on the door sound like the beating of a clock or a heart. . . . *Tick—tick*—like the heart that kept pulsing under the

floor in the famous and awful story, and when we were listening to it being done on the radio years ago, Mother said 'Turn it off'" (124).

18. Rachel describes the scene as follows:

> The chapel in the blue light is as squarely shaped and unhaunted as it would be at high noon. The pews are blonde wood, of an extreme sheen, and at the front there is a platform of the same sleek blonde, the right height for placing the burden without undue strain on the pall-bearers. . . . On low tables at either side are set candelabra as many-branched as trees, and the wax tapers in them are violet and peppermint green. The walls are done in simulated pine, paper printed with wood knots. (131-32)

19. The ritualized funeral service carried out by Hector Jonas is an echo of elegiac tradition, as was the representation of the grave-yard in the opening scenes of *The Stone Angel*. In Milton's "Lycidas," a procession of mourners is figured by the elegist, as is a funeral bier, replete with flowers. Likewise, in Shelley's "Adonais," a procession of mourners visits Adonais's death chamber, along with the elegist himself. In both cases, the procession and the representations of the dead are purely drama-tized events for the purposes of allowing the elegists to carry out an aspect of their work of mourning. Additionally, in both elegies, once the procession of mourners has passed, the consola-tory movement of the elegy occurs. Laurence emphasizes the dramatic qualities of Rachel's visit to the funeral parlour, as Hector acts as stage manager to her personal theatre, and the setting itself, with its highly artificial backdrop and the back-ground music, reinforces this.

20. Stovel, *Rachel's Children*, 47.

CHAPTER THREE

1. James King notes that the title of the novel is "an apocalyptic metaphor for all human beings, all victims of a media-driven, vio-lence-prone world. . . . Life is hell, the title suggests—or, at the very least, a purgatory." See *The Life of Margaret Laurence*, 249.

2. Freud, "Mourning and Melancholia."

3. Nora Stovel, *Stacey's Choice: Margaret Laurence's 'The Fire-Dwellers'* (Toronto: ECW Press, 1993), 38.

4. Cited by Ronald Shleifer, *Rhetoric and Death: The Language of Modernism and Postmodern Discourse Theory* (Urbana and Chicago: The University of Illinois Press, 1990), 1-2.

5. My discussion of the denial of death in the previous chapter applies to Stacey's scenario as well.

6. Jahan Ramazani, *Poetry of Mourning: The Modern Elegy From Hardy to Heaney* (Chicago and London: University of Chicago Press, 1994), 14.

7. To echo Derrida, it is difficult to accord oneself the right to mourn in a society that publicly defines that mourning as a transgressive act.

8. Ramazani notes in *Poetry of Mourning:* "The modern elegy enables the work of mourning in the face of social suppression, but it also instances that suppression" (16).

9. I would like to thank Birk Sproxton for pointing out that the "other city" referred to is named on page 250 as Hiroshima.

10. While perhaps Romantic in nature, in part, Stacey's nostalgic yearning for an ideal past is partially rooted in her own positive experiences. Phyllis Grosskurth notes in "Wise and Gentle" that "[Stacey's] favourite day-dream is of herself as a teenager jiving with joyous abandonment" (in *Margaret Laurence: The Writer and Her Critics*, ed. W.H. New [Toronto: McGraw-Hill Ryerson, 1997], 227).

11. Her only negative memories of rural space are linked to Manawaka—a place which, after all, she was able to escape successfully.

12. Near the opening of "Lycidas," Milton depicts the "high lawns" of the shared past and the magical place where "Rough satyrs danced, and fauns with cloven heel / from the glad sound would not absent long / And old Damoetas loved to hear our song." In remembering the glory of the countryside around Oxford (which is depicted as a Greek pastoral space), Arnold writes, ". . . leafless, yet soft as spring, / The tender purple spray on copse and briers! / And that sweet city with her dreaming spires, / She needs not June for beauty's heightening." When he describes Thyrsis's departure from the pastoral countryside, the negativity of the

contrast is clear: "He went; his piping took a troubled sound / Of storms that rage outside our happy ground; / He could not wait their passing. . . ." Shelley notes that in death Adonais is protected "From the contagion of the world's slow stain."

13. The echoes of Wordsworth's "Lines Composed a Few Miles Above Tintern Abbey" are evident, too, as the narrator of that poem seeks solace in the happy memories of the countryside as a respite from the "din" of city life.

14. Nora Stovel, "Female Excalibur as Literary Legacy: Ethel Wilson's *Swamp Angel* and Margaret Laurence's *The Fire-Dwellers*," *The International Fiction Review* 21 (1994): 30; Allan Bevan, "Introduction," in Margaret Laurence, *The Fire-Dwellers* (Toronto: McClelland and Stewart, 1973), xi.

15. The symbolism of the burn ties into the whole notion of the consuming fire. Here, the fire has crossed over the boundary from threat to action, the symbolic flames of the "scarlet circle" singeing her. Allan Bevan notes in his introduction to *The Fire-Dwellers*, "The pervading image of fire, in many forms, is usually related to Stacey's state of mind" (xi), and Stovel sees the novel as being "Framed by fire." See *Stacey's Choice*, 94. Other critics, too, note the centrality of fire imagery to Stacey's life. Sharon Nancekevill, in *"The Fire-Dwellers*: Circles of Fire," *The Literary Criterion* 19 (1984): 124-31, sees a cyclical nature to the use of fire in the novel, and Miriam Packer, in "The Dance of Life: *The Fire-Dwellers*," *Journal of Canadian Fiction* 27 (1980): 124-31, explores the pervasiveness of fire symbols.

16. The *Concise Oxford Dictionary* defines "venture" as "an undertaking of a risk" and as "a risky undertaking." Certainly, by being forced to confront and express her emotions, Stacey ventures into risky terrain. The *Oxford English Dictionary* cites "aventure" from the French, meaning adventure, as a source for "venture."

17. In a further moment Stacey imagines the polarities of choice (chaotic life versus simple life) that she has: "I have to get away sometimes. I have to. I'm trapped. I have to see Luke. I have to. Too many people here, too many crises I don't know how to deal with, too much yakkity-yak from all of us, too few words that tell any of us a damn thing about any of the others. With Luke everything is simple" (194).

18. The driving here counters earlier patterns where Stacey drives dangerously and automatically. Now, she is in control, "driving" *him* in his grief.

19. I use the word "control" deliberately here as Stacey is attempting to impose rigidity on her scene as if to say, "This is the code I will live by: No pre-mourning."

CHAPTER FOUR

1. I will refer to *A Bird in the House* as a novel. Criticism of *A Bird in the House* has frequently concerned itself with structure and form. As a series of eight linked stories, but as not quite definitely a novel like the other texts in the Manawaka series, the book has confounded precise generic definition. *A Bird in the House* cannot accurately be defined as a collection of stories because of the interrelationship of the individual pieces; as critic Bruce Stovel points out, "the artistry in each story lies in the interconnected, cumulative resonances that bind the stories together into a single, coherent whole." See "Coherence in Margaret Laurence's *A Bird in the House*," *Anglo-American Studies* 9, 2 (1989): 130. Jon Kertzer perhaps best expresses some of these concerns when he argues that "it does not matter whether we treat . . . [Vanessa's recollections] as a collection of stories or novel with eight chapters. In either case the book aspires to a special kind of unity." See *"That House in Manawaka"*: *Margaret Laurence's* A Bird in the House (Toronto: ECW Press, 1992), 22.

2. Arnold E. Davidson, "Cages and Escapes in Margaret Laurence's *A Bird in the House*," *University of Windsor Review* 16 (1981): 100.

3. Kertzer, *"That House in Manawaka,"* 80. Other critics, too, have noticed the importance of structuring actions within Vanessa's activity of narrative-creation. As Michael Darling remarks, Vanessa "is trying to order her past, with the understanding that art can improve upon life in the imposition of order upon chaos." See "'Undecipherable Signs': Margaret Laurence's 'To Set Our House in Order'," *Essays on Canadian Writing* 29 (1984): 199. Remarking upon the manner with which the story "To Set Our House in Order" is told, W.J. Keith points out that "Laurence, in making Vanessa tell her story in this particular way, has enabled her to set her house in order." See *A Sense of Style: Studies in the*

Art of Fiction in English-Speaking Canada (Toronto: ECW Press, 1989), 117.

4. Milton in "Lycidas," Shelley in "Adonais," and Arnold in "Thyrsis," as with Dryden in "In Memory of Mr. Oldham," present narrators who repeatedly make statements about the poem they are composing and/or reciting and especially note the difficult process of dealing with the loss of their loved one through the means of writing.

5. In "Adonais," for example, the elegist depicts a procession of mourners who are unable to grieve effectively.

6. I look at five of the eight stories, as they are the ones that deal with the loss of family members: "The Sound of the Singing," "A Bird in the House," "To Set Our House in Order," "The Mask of the Bear," and "Jericho's Brick Battlements."

7. Smythe, *Figuring Grief*, 130.

8. Kertzer, *"That House in Manawaka,"* 23.

9. Ibid., 24.

10. Darling, "Undecipherable Signs," 192.

CHAPTER FIVE

1. Nora Stovel, *"(W)rites of Passage:* The Typescript of *The Diviners* as Shadow Text," in *Margaret Laurence: Critical Reflections,* ed. David Staines (Ottawa: University of Ottawa Press, 2001), 101.

2. *The Diviners* has consistently been read by literary critics in relation to issues of Morag's exploration of her identity—in terms of her past and present family and cultural background. Eleanor Johnston terms Morag's actions "divination": "the search for something of 'value'." See "The Quest of *The Diviners,*" *Mosaic* 11, 3 (1978): 107-121; and Thomas Jefferson specifies the "value" in the sense of "a literary quest for Canadian cultural identity," which is expressed as an "obsession with family." See "Biblical Hermeneutic and Family History in Contemporary Canadian Fiction: Wiebe and Laurence," *Mosaic* 11, 3 (1978): 87. Other critics have specified the exploration of identity as a Jungian process of individuation. Angelika Maeser Lemieux comments that "The experience of autogenesis or self-creation constitutes the core of Laurence's stories." See "Finding the Mother: The

Individuation of Laurence's Heroines," *Journal of Canadian Fiction*, 27 (1980): 151; and Terry Goldie states that Morag is "going through a search for identity, what Jung referred to as individuation, 'becoming one's own self'." He further elucidates this theme: "In *The Diviners*, there is this feeling that while the quest for identity requires an exploration of the past it must also be shaped by the present and by those a sociologist would call the 'significant others,' parents, children, lovers, and friends." See his "Folklore, Popular Culture and Individuation in *Surfacing* and *The Diviners*," *Canadian Literature* 104 (1985): 95. In a similar vein, Barbara Godard remarks, "In mid-life crisis, with her daughter leaving home, Morag Gunn is engaged in the process of individuation." See "*The Diviners* as Supplement: (M)othering the Text," *Open Letter* 7, 7 (1990): 34.

3. Paul Hjartarson notes that the stories Morag tells in her narrative are "intended to fill the void left by the loss of her parents." See "'Christie's Real Country. Where I was Born': Story-Telling, Loss and Subjectivity in *The Diviners*," in *Crossing the River: Essays in Honour of Margaret Laurence*, ed. Kristjana Gunnars (Winnipeg: Turnstone Press, 1989), 49. Barbara Godard points out that a void in Morag's life is at the centre of the novel: "At the core of the story is an absence; quest for this absence is the only presence." See "*The Diviners* as Supplement," 34-55. Méira Cook remarks that "The novel that Morag is writing . . . begins with her daughter's absence . . . [and] the incidence of parental loss precipitates this narrative"; for Morag, "story is her only consolation against death, a constructed presence that stands in for inconsolable absence." See "Becoming the Mother: Construction of the Maternal in *The Diviners*," in *Challenging Territory: The Writing of Margaret Laurence*, ed. Christian Riegel (Edmonton: University of Alberta Press, 1997), 87, 90.

Criticism of *The Diviners* has been quick to recognize the overt role that Laurence has given to the contemplation of the act of writing itself. W.H. New points out, "By making Morag a writer, by making Morag so deliberately reconstruct a life, [Laurence] draws our attention to the process of fabrication." See *Margaret Laurence*, 79. In a similar vein, Susan Warwick remarks that there is "an over-riding sense that this is a novel in process, a work in which the telling of stories is as important as the stories told, and in which the very act of telling a story confers meaning upon past, present, and future experience. . . . A reading of *The Diviners* as both fiction by Laurence and fiction by the novel's central character and narrator makes clear that one of the novel's main concerns is the nature of fiction, of the written word." See *The River of Now and Then: The Diviners* (Toronto: ECW Press, 1993), 19. Similarly, Gayle Greene comments that Morag "uses her fiction to make her way in the world and to make sense of the world," and that "the 'creative process' is . . . so deeply 'worked into the narrative' that all Morag's efforts to remember, reconstruct and revise the past are problems relating to narrative." See "Margaret Laurence's *The Diviners*: The Uses of the Past," in *Critical Approaches to the Fiction of Margaret Laurence*, ed. Colin Nicholson (Vancouver: University of British Columbia Press, 1990), 179, 182. Ildiko de Papp Carrington notes, "Laurence dramatizes in detail the creative processes by which 'facts' become fictionalized, by which life, lived and remembered, is not simply recorded but intellectually and emotionally reinterpreted in successive stages of time and imaginatively transmuted not only from one narrative form to another but also from one point of view to another." See "'Tales in the Telling': *The Diviners* as Fiction About Fiction," *ECW* 9 (1977-78): 168. J.A. Wainwright notes that in *The Diviners* the artist "investigate[s] the relationship between her art and her life." See "'You Have to Go Home Again': Art and Life in *The Diviners*," *World Literature Written in English* 20, 2 (1981): 193.

4. Esther Rashkin, "A Recipe For Mourning: Isak Dinesen's 'Babette's Feast'," *Style* 29, 3 (1995): 357.

5. Paul Hjartarson argues convincingly that the narrative of the past, what he identifies as the "Then" narrative, is "embedded in and subordinate to the Now" narrative—what I have termed the frame-text. To view the narrative that makes up the whole of *The Diviners* in this way is to acknowledge that the frame-text presents information integral to an understanding of the book as a whole: "To privilege the Now narrative is to view Morag in terms of her present life, to conceive her in the process of understanding herself. The one views self as product; the other, as process." See "Christie's Real Country," 63, 47.

6. Richard Stamelman, *Lost Beyond Telling*, 7.

7. Ferdinand de Saussure originated the use of signifier and signified in relation to the linguistic sign. A signifier, writes Gerald Prince, is "a socially constituted entity linking a perceptible image and a concept," which is the signified, and "neither exists outside of its relation with the other." Gerald Prince, *A Dictionary of Narratology* (Lincoln and London: University of Nebraska Press, 1987), 87. See de Saussure's *Course in General Linguistics*, trans. Wade Baskin (New York: McGraw-Hill, 1966), 65-70.

8. Morag has an indirect experience of the physical attributes of corpses when she is a child when Christie describes the foetus he buried in the Nuisance Grounds as being "like a skinned rabbit" (87).

9. Beatrice Martina Guenther, *The Poetics of Death: The Short Prose of Kleist and Balzac* (Albany: The State University of New York Press, 1996), 59.

10. Hjartarson, "Christie's Real Country," 60.

11. Barbara Godard, "Caliban's Revolt: The Discourses of the (M)other," in *Critical Approaches to the Fiction of Margaret Laurence*, ed. Colin Nicholson (Vancouver: University of British Columbia Press, 1990), 35.

12. Méira Cook notes, "What [Morag] mourns initially is not the fact of their deaths but the loss of an iconography, signalled by the absence in the scopic field of any appropriate referent." See "Becoming the Mother," 87.

13. Buss, *Mother and Daughter Relationships*, 67.

14. Marcienne Rocard, "The Dispossession Theme in Margaret Laurence's *The Diviners*," *World Literature Written in English* 21, 1 (1982): 111.

15. Robert Kastenbaum outlines five approaches to helping children cope with bereavement: "Develop and maintain an open communication pattern with children"; "Give children the opportunity to choose attending the funeral"; "Encourage the expression of feelings"; "Provide convincing assurance that there will always be somebody to love and look after the child"; "Professional counselling should be considered if the bereaved children are at special risk." See *Death, Society, and Human Experience*, 211-12.

16. Interestingly, all the bodies Morag has knowledge of have been

167

compared to animals in some form or another: the discarded baby was described as appearing like a skinned rabbit, Piquette and her children are figured as roasted meat, and her parents are thought of as gophers run over by a car.

17. Morag reflects on the effects of Dieppe on Manawaka, puncturing the romantic artifice of the propaganda and the First World War poetry she has been exposed to:

> The news of Dieppe changes the town of Manawaka. It will never be the same again. Not until this moment has the War been a reality here. Now it is a reality. There are many dead who will not be buried in the Manawaka cemetery up on the hill where the tall spruces stand like dark angels. There are a great many families who now have fewer sons, or none. (158)

Morag is well aware of the human cost of war—"The only truth at the moment seems to be in the long lists of the dead. The only certainty is that they are dead. Forever and ever and ever" (159)—but the reaction of society is to attempt to soften the blow of death, to turn it into something that is worth happening. As Morag remembers, "The newspapers for days are full of stories of bravery, courage, camaraderie, initiative, heroism, gallantry, and determination in the face of enemy fire" (159). From this experience, Morag muses about the nature of stories, for she wonders about the verity of what she reads: "Are any of the stories true? . . . What is a story? Is there any such thing?" (159). In these considerations, Morag realizes that the stories have a specific function or role to play in the lives of the bereaved: "They may console some," she thinks (159), and the truth "does not matter" (159) in this case. This is an important lesson for Morag, because she learns that stories can bring much-needed consolation to those who suffer loss, although she is not certain that skirting around or obscuring the horror of the truth is the way to go about consoling oneself.

18. In his *Poetics*, Aristotle theorizes the concept of recognition, or *anagnorisis*. Terence Cave notes, "anagnorisis brings about a shift from ignorance to knowledge; it is the moment at which the characters understand their predicament fully for the first time." Recognition is, he continues, "the sense of a means of knowing which is different from rational cognition. It operates

surreptitiously, randomly, [and] elliptically." See *Recognitions: A Study in Poetics* (Oxford: Clarendon Press, 1988), 1,3.

19. Morag's conception of Prin as having been dead in spirit for some years before her biological death approximates the definition of social death in sociology. Michael Mulkay states that

> any particular death sequence comes to an end when an individual's actual or impending biological or clinical death is taken as grounds for treating that individual as a non-person. By 'non-person' I mean that the actor has ceased to exist as an active agent in the ongoing social world of some other party. When social death has occurred, other people no longer seek to communicate with that person nor take that person directly into account in carrying out their own actions.

See "Social Death in Britain," in *The Sociology of Death: Theory, Culture, Practice*, ed. David Clark (Oxford: Blackwell/*The Sociological Review*, 1993), 33.

20. Later, Christie voices his own resistance to the funerary rituals sanctioned by the community: "If I'd had it up to me. . . . I would have buried her my own self. . . . In the Nuisance Grounds" (274-75), he says. Christie is voicing the individual needs of survivors to grieve the dead in their own personal ways.

21. Jerusalem the golden
With milk and honey blest—
They stand, those halls of Sion
All jubilant with song,
And bright with many an angel,
And all the martyr throng;
The Prince is ever in them,
The daylight is serene,
The pastures of the blessèd

22. Brooke Skelton emigrated from England and had his own colonial background, having lived a life of privilege in India as a child.

23. I would like to thank Nora Stovel and Birk Sproxton for making this connection evident to me.

24. Her reactions here are similar to those described in the literature of mourning and bereavement. Stephen Schuchter points out that the initial reactions to loss "include an initial period of shock followed by intense emotional pangs of grief. The 'shock' may be experienced as a sense of numbness or unreality, it may have a dreamlike quality, or it may be a state of normal thinking and functioning. In this state of detachment, the individual is protected from the impact of a new reality" (2). For clinical accounts of the acute reactions to loss see E. Lindemann, "Symptomatology and Management of Acute Grief," *American Journal of Psychiatry* 101 (1944): 141-49; C.M. Parkes, "The First Year of Bereavement: A Longitudinal Study of the Reaction of London Widows to the Death of Their Husbands," *Psychiatry* 33 (1970): 444-67; I.O. Glick, C.M. Parkes, and R. Weiss, *The First Year of Bereavement* (New York: Basic Books, 1975).

25. Morag is faced with the glitzy businesslike nature of the funeral when she approaches the sign at what used to be Cameron's Funeral Home: "It is now an enormous crimson neon, letters about a million feet high, and it would appear at first glance to apply to some publicity-worshiping evangelical sect" (422).

26. "Nuisance Grounds" is the town's name for the town garbage dump, where Christie discovers the many secrets of upstanding members of Manawaka society. "Nuisance" refers to the effect the grounds have on Manawaka society.

27. The exchange is as follows:

"Do you think he'll see me, Billy?"
"Yeh. I think so."
"He didn't say he wanted to see me?"
"Well, no. But—" (466)

AFTERWORD

1. Jahan Ramazani, *Poetry of Mourning: The Modern Elegy from Hardy to Heaney* (Chicago and London: University of Chicago Press, 1994), 29.

2. Kathleen Woodward, "Late Theory, Late Style: Loss and Renewal in Freud and Barthes," in *Aging and Gender in Literature: Studies in Creativity*, ed. Anne M. Brown and Janice Rossin (Charlottesville and London: University Press of Virginia, 1993), 83, 85.

3. All three plants are associated with poetic inspiration.

4. Lycidas is Milton's name for Edward King, who drowned off the English coast.

5. Ramazani, *Poetry of Mourning*, 1.

6. Ibid., 3.

7. For a full discussion of the role of the cenotaph in *The Fire-Dwellers*, see Birk Sproxton's insightful essay "The Figure of the Unknown Soldier: Home and War in *The Fire-Dwellers*," in *Margaret Laurence: Critical Reflections*, ed. David Staines (Ottawa: University of Ottawa Press, 2001), 79-100.

8. Arthur W. Frank, *The Wounded Storyteller: Body, Illness, and Ethics* (Chicago and London: The University of Chicago Press, 1995), xi.

BIBLIOGRAPHY

Ariès, Philip. *The Hour of Our Death*. Trans. Helen Weaver. New York: Knopf, 1981.

_____. *Western Attitudes Towards Death: From the Middle Ages to the Present*. Trans. Patricia M. Ranum. Baltimore and London: Johns Hopkins University Press, 1974.

Aristotle. *Poetics*. Trans. James Hutton. New York: Norton, 1982.

Arnold, Matthew. "Dover Beach." In *The Norton Anthology of English Literature*. Fifth Ed. Gen. ed. M.H. Abrams. New York: W.W. Norton, 1987, 2132-33.

_____. "Thyrsis." In *The Norton Anthology of English Literature*. Fifth Ed. Gen. ed. M.H. Abram. New York: W.W. Norton, 1987, 2139-46.

Attig, Thomas. *How We Grieve: Relearning the World*. New York: Oxford University Press, 1996.

Bailey, Nancy. "Psychology of Re-birth in *A Jest of God*." *Journal of Popular Culture* 15 (1981): 62-67.

Bakhtin, Mikhail M. *The Dialogic Imagination*. Trans. and ed. Caryl Emerson and Michael Holquist. Texas: University of Texas Press, 1981.

_____. *Problems of Dostoevsky's Poetics*. Trans. and ed. Caryl Emerson. Minneapolis: University of Minnesota Press, 1984.

Barsky, Robert F. and Michael Holquist, eds. *Bakhtin and Otherness. Discours social/Social Discourse: International Research Papers in Comparative Literature*. Vol. 3.1 & 3.2 (1990).

Barthes, Roland. "An Introduction to the Structural Analysis of Narrative." *New Literary History* 6 (1975): 237-62.

Becker, Ernst. *The Denial of Death*. New York: The Free Press, 1973.

Beckman-Long, Brenda. "*The Stone Angel* as a Feminine Confessional Novel." In *Challenging Territory: The Writing of Margaret Laurence*. Ed. Christian Riegel. Edmonton: University of Alberta Press, 1997, 47-66.

Bell, Alice. "Hagar Shipley's Rage for Life: Narrative Technique in *The Stone Angel*." In *New Perspectives on the Writing of Margaret Laurence: Poetic Narrative, Multiculturalism, and Feminism*. Ed. Greta M.K. Coger. Westport and London: Greenwood Press, 1996, 51-62.

Benveniste, Emile. *Problèmes de linguistique générale II*. Paris: Gallimard, 1974.

Bevan, Allan. "Introduction." *The Fire-Dwellers*. NCL. Toronto: McClelland and Stewart, 1973, viii-xiv.

Bök, Christian. "Sibyls: Echoes of French Feminism in *The Diviners* and *Lady Oracle*." *Canadian Literature* 135 (1992): 80-93.

Bowering, George. "That Fool of a Fear: Notes on *A Jest of God*." In *A Place to Stand On: Essays by and about Margaret Laurence*. Ed. George Woodcock. Edmonton: NeWest Press, 1983, 210-26.

Bowlby, John. *Loss: Sadness and Depression*. London: Pimlico, 1980.

_____. *Separation: Anger and Anxiety*. London: Pimlico, 1973. Reprinted 1998.

Buss, Helen M. *Mother and Daughter Relationships in the Manawaka Works of Margaret Laurence*. English Literary Studies. Victoria: University of Victoria, 1985.

Carse, James P. *Death and Existence: A Conceptual History of Human Mortality*. New York: John Wiley and Sons, 1980.

Cave, Terence. *Recognitions: A Study in Poetics*. Oxford: Clarendon, 1988. Reprinted 1990.

Chew, Shirley. "'Some Truer Image': A Reading of *The Stone Angel*." In *Critical Approaches to the Writing of Margaret Laurence*. Ed. Colin Nicholson. Vancouver: University of British Columbia Press, 1990, 35-45.

Clark, David, ed. *The Sociology of Death: Theory, Culture, Practice.* Oxford: Blackwell / *The Sociological Review,* 1993.

Clark, David. "Introduction." In *The Sociology of Death: Theory, Culture, Practice.* Ed. David Clark. Oxford: Blackwell / *The Sociological Review,* 1993, 3-10.

Clayton, John J. *Gestures of Healing: Anxiety and the Modern Novel.* Amherst: The University of Massachusetts Press, 1991.

Coger, Greta M.K., ed. *New Perspectives on Margaret Laurence: Poetic Narrative, Multiculturalism, and Feminism.* Westport and London: Greenwood Press, 1996.

Cole, Susan Letzer. *The Absent One: Mourning Ritual, Tragedy, and the Performance of Ambivalence.* University Park and London: The Pennsylvania State University Press, 1985.

Cook, Méira. "Becoming the Mother: Constructions of the Maternal in *The Diviners.*" In *Challenging Territory: The Writing of Margaret Laurence.* Ed. Christian Riegel. Edmonton: The University of Alberta Press, 1997, 81-98.

Crenshaw, David A. *Bereavement: Counseling the Grieving Throughout the Life Cycle.* New York: Continuum Press, 1990.

Culler, Jonathan. *Structuralist Poetics: Structuralism, Linguistics and the Study of Literature.* London: Routledge and Kegan Paul, 1975.

Darling, Michael. "'Undecipherable Signs': Margaret Laurence's 'To Set Our House in Order.'" *Essays on Canadian Writing* 29 (1984): 192-203.

Davey, Frank. *Post-National Arguments: The Politics of the Anglophone-Canadian Novel Since 1967.* Toronto: University of Toronto Press, 1993.

Davidson, Arnold E. "Cages and Escapes in Margaret Laurence's *A Bird in the House.*" *University of Windsor Review* 16 (1981): 92-201.

Davies, Richard. "'Half War/Half Peace': Margaret Laurence and the Publishing of *A Bird in the House.*" *English Studies in Canada* 17, 3 (1991): 337-46.

de Papp Carrington, Ildikó. "'Tales in the Telling': *The Diviners* as Fiction about Fiction." *ECW* 9 (1977-78): 154-69.

Derrida, Jacques. *The Work of Mourning*. Ed. and trans. Pascale-Anne Brault and Michael Naas. Chicago and London: University of Chicago Press, 2001.

DeSpelder, Ann Lynne, and Albert Lee Strickland. *The Last Dance: Encountering Death and Dying*. Mountain View: Mayfield Publishing, 1996.

Dombrowski, Theo Quayle. "Word and Fact: Laurence and Language." *Canadian Literature* 80 (1979): 50-62.

Donnelly, John. *Language, Metaphysics, and Death*. New York: Fordham University Press, 1978.

Dryden, John. "In Memory of Mr. Oldham." In *The Norton Anthology of English Literature*. Fifth Ed. Gen. ed. M.H. Abrams. New York: W.W. Norton, 1987, 882-83.

Fabré, Michel. "The Angel and Living Water: Metaphorical Networks and Structural Opposition in *The Stone Angel*." In *New Perspectives on the Writing of Margaret Laurence: Poetic Narrative, Multiculturalism, and Feminism*. Ed. Greta M.K. Coger. Westport and London: Greenwood Press, 1996, 17-28.

Firmat, Gustavo Pérez. *Literature and Liminality: Festive Readings in the Hispanic Tradition*. Durham: Duke University Press, 1986.

Frank, Arthur W. *The Wounded Storyteller: Body, Illness, and Ethics*. Chicago and London: University of Chicago Press, 1995.

Franks, Jill. "Jesting Within: Voices of Irony and Parody as Expressions of Feminisms." In *Challenging Territory: The Writing of Margaret Laurence*. Ed. Christian Riegel. Edmonton: University of Alberta Press, 1997, 99-118.

Freud, Sigmund. "Mourning and Melancholia." In *A General Selection from the Works of Sigmund Freud*. Ed. John Rickman. Garden City: Doubleday, 1957, 124-40.

Fulton, Robert. *Death and Identity*. New York: John Wiley, 1965.

Genette, Gérard. *Narrative Discourse*. Trans. J. Lewin. Ithaca and London: Cornell University Press, 1980.

Gervais, Karen Grandstrand. *Redefining Death*. New Haven and London: Yale University Press, 1986.

Glick, I.O., C.M. Parkes, and R. Weiss. *The First Year of Bereavement*. New York: Basic Books, 1975.

Godard, Barbara. "Caliban's Revolt: The Discourses of the (M)other." In *Critical Approaches to the Writing of Margaret Laurence*. Ed. Colin Nicholson. Vancouver: University of British Columbia Press, 1990, 208-227.

_____. "*The Diviners* as Supplement: (M)othering the Text." *Open Letter* 7, 7 (1990): 26-73.

Goldie, Terry. "Folklore, Popular Culture and Individuation in *Surfacing* and *The Diviners*." *Canadian Literature* 104 (1985): 95-110.

Gorer, Geoffrey. *Death, Grief and Mourning in Contemporary Britain*. Garden City, NJ: Doubleday, 1965.

Gray, Thomas. "Elegy Written in a Country Church-Yard." In *The Broadview Anthology of Poetry*. Ed. Herbert Rosengarten and Amanda Goldrick-Jones. Peterborough: Broadview Press, 1993, 131-34.

Greimas, A.J. "Narrative Grammar: Units and Levels." *Modern Language Notes* 86 (1971): 795-806.

Greene, Gayle. "Margaret Laurence's *The Diviners*: The Uses of the Past." In *Critical Approaches to the Writing of Margaret Laurence*. Ed. Colin Nicholson. Vancouver: University of British Columbia Press, 1990, 177-207.

Grimes, Ronald L. *Beginnings in Ritual Studies*. Rev. ed. Columbia: University of South Carolina Press, 1995.

Grosskurth, Phyllis. "Wise and Gentle." In *Margaret Laurence: The Writer and Her Critics*. Ed. W.H. New. Toronto: McGraw-Hill Ryerson, 1977, 227-28.

Guenther, Beatrice Martina. *The Poetics of Death: The Short Prose of Kleist and Balzac*. Albany: The State University of New York Press, 1996.

BIBLIOGRAPHY

Gunnars, Kristjana, ed. *Crossing the River: Essays in Honour of Margaret Laurence*. Winnipeg: Turnstone Press, 1988.

Hardy, Thomas. "The Darkling Thrush." In *The Norton Anthology of English Literature*. Fifth Ed. Gen. ed. M.H. Abrams. New York: W.W. Norton, 1987, 2210-11.

Hjartarson, Paul. "'Christie's Real Country. Where I was Born': Story-Telling, Loss and Subjectivity in *The Diviners*." In *Crossing the River: Essays in Honour of Margaret Laurence*. Ed. Kristjana Gunnars. Winnipeg: Turnstone Press, 1988, 43-64.

Howarth, Glennys. "Investigating Deathwork: a personal account." In *The Sociology of Death: Theory, Culture, Practice*. Ed. David Clark. Oxford: Blackwell / *The Sociological Review*, 1993, 221-37.

Jefferson, Thomas. "Biblical Hermeneutic and Family History in Contemporary Canadian Fiction: Wiebe and Laurence." *Mosaic* 11, 3 (1978): 87-106.

Johnston, Eleanor, "The Quest of *The Diviners*." *Mosaic* 11, 3 (1978): 107-21.

Kastenbaum, Robert. *Death, Society, and Human Experience*. Fifth Ed. Boston: Allyn and Bacon, 1995.

Keith, W.J. *A Sense of Style: Studies in the Art of Fiction in English-Speaking Canada*. Toronto: ECW Press, 1989.

Kertzer, J.M. *'That House in Manawaka': Margaret Laurence's* A Bird in the House. Toronto: ECW Press, 1992.

_____. "*The Stone Angel*: Time and Responsibility." *The Dalhousie Review* 54, 3 (1972): 499-508.

King, James. *The Life of Margaret Laurence*. Toronto: Knopf, 1997.

Kübler-Ross, Elizabeth. *On Death and Dying*. London: Macmillan, 1969.

Lampkin, Loretta M. "An Interview with John Barth." *Contemporary Literature* 29 (1988): 488.

Laurence, Margaret. *A Bird in the House*. NCL. McClelland and Stewart, 1970. Reprinted 1989.

_____. *A Jest of God*. NCL. Toronto: McClelland and Stewart, 1966. Reprinted 1988.

_____. *Dance on the Earth: A Memoir*. Toronto: McClelland and Stewart, 1989.

_____. *The Diviners*. NCL. Toronto: McClelland and Stewart, 1974. Reprinted 1991.

_____. *The Fire-Dwellers*. NCL. Toronto: McClelland and Stewart, 1969. Reprinted 1990.

_____. *The Stone Angel*. NCL. Toronto: McClelland and Stewart, 1964. Reprinted 1995.

_____. "Time and the Narrative Voice." In *A Place to Stand On: Essays by and about Margaret Laurence*. Ed. George Woodcock. Edmonton: NeWest Press, 1983, 155-59.

Lentricchia, Frank, and Thomas McLaughlin, eds. *Critical Terms for Literary Study*. Chicago and London: The University of Chicago Press, 1990.

Lindemann, E. "Symptomatology and Management of Acute Grief." *American Journal of Psychiatry* 101 (1944): 141-49.

Maeser Lemieux, Angelika. "Finding the Mother: The Individuation of Laurence's Heroines." *Journal of Canadian Fiction* 27 (1980): 15-66.

Marris, Peter. *Loss and Change*. Garden City: Anchor Press/Doubleday, 1975.

Martin, Mathew. "Dramas of Desire in Margaret Laurence's *A Jest of God*, *The Fire-Dwellers*, and *The Diviners*." *Studies in Canadian Literature* 22, 1 (1995): 58-71.

McClellan, William. "The Dialogic Other: Bakhtin's Theory of Rhetoric." In *Bakhtin and Otherness. Discours social / Social Discourse: International Research Papers in Comparative Literature*. Vol. 3.1 & 3.2. Ed. Robert F. Barsky and Michael Holquist (1990): 233-47.

Mellor, David. "Death in High Modernity: The Contemporary Presence and Absence of Death." In *The Sociology of Death: Theory, Culture, Practice*. Ed. David Clark. Oxford: Blackwell / *The Sociological Review*, 1993, 11-30.

Milton, John. "Lycidas." In *The Norton Anthology of English Literature*. Fifth Ed. Gen. ed. M.H. Abrams. New York: W.W. Norton, 1987. 658-64.

Mitchell, W.J.T. "Representation." In *Critical Terms for Literary Study*. Ed. Frank Lentricchi and Thomas McLaughlin. Chicago and London: The University of Chicago Press, 1990, 11-22.

Morawski, Jill J. *Practising Feminisms, Reconstructing Psychology: Notes on a Liminal Science*. Ann Arbor: The University of Michigan Press, 1994.

Mulkay, Michael. "Social Death in Britain." In *The Sociology of Death: Theory, Culture, Practice*. Ed. David Clark. Oxford: Blackwell / *The Sociological Review*, 1993, 31-49.

Nancekevill, Sharon. "*The Fire-Dwellers*: Circles of Fire." *The Literary Criterion* 19 (1984): 124-31.

New, W.H., ed. *Margaret Laurence: The Writer and Her Critics*. Toronto: McGraw-Hill Ryerson, 1977.

Nicholson, Colin, ed. *Critical Approaches to the Fiction of Margaret Laurence*. Vancouver: University of British Columbia Press, 1990.

Packer, Miriam. "The Dance of Life: *The Fire-Dwellers*." *Journal of Canadian Fiction* 27 (1980): 124-31.

Parkes, C.M. "The First Year of Bereavement: A Longitudinal Study of the Reaction of London Widows to the Death of Their Husbands." *Psychiatry* 33 (1970): 444-67.

Pitkin, Hanna Fenichel, ed. *Representation*. New York: Atherton Press, 1969.

Powell, Barbara. "The Conflicting Inner Voices of Rachel Cameron." *Studies in Canadian Literature* 16, 1 (1984): 22-35.

Prince, Gerald. *A Dictionary of Narratology*. Lincoln and London: University of Nebraska Press, 1987.

Ramazani, Jahan. *Poetry of Mourning: The Modern Elegy From Hardy to Heaney*. Chicago and London: University of Chicago Press, 1994.

Rando, Therese A. *Grief, Dying, and Death: Clinical Interventions for Caregivers*. Champaign, Ill: Research Press, 1984.

Raphael, Beverly. *The Anatomy of Bereavement*. New York: Basic Books, 1983.

Rashkin, Esther. "A Recipe for Mourning: Isak Dinesen's 'Babette's Feast'." *Style* 29, 3 (1995): 356-74.

Riegel, Christian, ed. *Challenging Territory: The Writing of Margaret Laurence*. Edmonton: University of Alberta Press, 1997.

Rimmon-Kenan, Schlomith. *Narrative Fiction: Contemporary Poetics*. London: Routledge, 1983.

Rocard, Marcienne. "The Dispossession Theme in Margaret Laurence's *The Diviners*." *World Literature Written in English* 21, 1 (1982): 109-14.

Rooke, Constance. "Hagar's Old Age: *The Stone Angel as Vollendungsroman*." In *Crossing the River: Essays in Honour of Margaret Laurence*. Ed. Kristjana Gunnars. Winnipeg: Turnstone Press, 1988, 25-42.

Sacks, Peter M. *The English Elegy: Studies in the Genre from Spenser to Yeats*. Baltimore and London: The Johns Hopkins University Press, 1985.

de Saussure, Ferdinand. *Course in General Linguistics*. Trans. Wade Baskin. New York: McGraw-Hill, 1966.

Schleifer, Ronald. *Rhetoric and Death: The Language of Modernism and Postmodern Discourse Theory*. Urbana and Chicago: The University of Illinois Press, 1990.

Schuchter, Stephen R. *Dimensions of Grief: Adjusting to the Death of a Spouse*. San Francisco and London: Jossey-Bass Publishers, 1986.

Shapiro, Ester R. *Grief as a Family Process: A Developmental Approach to Clinical Practice.* New York and London: The Guilford Press, 1994.

Shelley, Percy Bysshe. "Adonais." In *The Norton Anthology of English Literature.* Fifth Ed. Gen. ed. M.H. Abram. New York: W.W. Norton, 1987, 1790-1803.

Shibles, Warren. *Death: An Interdisciplinary Analysis.* Whitewater: The Language Press, 1974.

Silverman, Kaja. *The Subject of Semiotics.* New York and Oxford: Oxford University Press, 1983.

Smythe, Karen E. *Figuring Grief: Gallant, Munro, and the Poetics of Elegy.* Montreal and Kingston: McGill-Queen's University Press, 1992.

Sproxton, Birk. "The Figure of the Unknown Soldier: Home and War in *The Fire-Dwellers.*" In *Margaret Laurence: Critical Reflections. Reappraisals: Canadian Writers.* Ed. David Staines. Ottawa: University of Ottawa Press, 2001, 79-100.

Staines, David, ed. *Margaret Laurence: Critical Reflections. Reappraisals: Canadian Writers.* Ottawa: University of Ottawa Press, 2001.

Stamelman, Richard. *Lost Beyond Telling: Representations of Death and Absence in Modern French Poetry.* Ithaca and London: Cornell University Press, 1990.

Stovel, Bruce. "Coherence in Margaret Laurence's *A Bird in the House.*" *Anglo-American Studies* 9, 2 (1989): 129-44.

Stovel, Nora Foster. "Female Excalibur as Literary Legacy: Ethel Wilson's *Swamp Angel* and Margaret Laurence's *The Fire-Dwellers.*" *The International Fiction Review* 21 (1994): 25-31.

_____. *Rachel's Children: Margaret Laurence's 'A Jest of God'.* Toronto: ECW Press, 1992.

_____. "Sisters Under Their Skins: *A Jest of God* and *The Fire-Dwellers.*" In *Challenging Territory: The Writing of Margaret Laurence.* Ed. Christian Riegel. Edmonton: University of Alberta Press, 1997, 119-38.

_____. *Stacey's Choice: Margaret Laurence's 'The Fire-Dwellers'*. Toronto: ECW Press, 1993.

_____. "*(W)rites of Passage:* The Typescript of *The Diviners* as Shadow Text." In *Margaret Laurence: Critical Reflections. Reappraisals: Canadian Writers*. Ed. David Staines. Ottawa: University of Ottawa Press, 2001, 101-20.

The Concise Oxford Dictionary. Oxford: Clarendon Press, 1990.

Tolchin, Neal L. *Mourning, Gender, and Creativity in the Art of Herman Melville*. New Haven and London: Yale University Press, 1993.

Turner, Victor. *The Anthropology of Performance*. New York: PAJ Publications, 1986.

_____. *Dramas, Fields, and Metaphors: Symbolic Action in Human Society*. New Ithaca and London: Cornell University Press, 1974.

_____. "Variations on a Theme of Liminality." In *Secular Ritual*. Ed. S.F. Moore and B.G. Meyerhoff. Amsterdam: Van Gorcum, 1977, 36-52.

van Gennep, Arnold. *The Rites of Passage*. Trans. Monika B. Vizedom and Gabrielle L. Caffee. Chicago: The University of Chicago Press, 1960.

van Herk, Aritha. "The Eulalias of Spinsters and Undertakers." In *Crossing the River: Essays in Honour of Margaret Laurence*. Ed. Kristjana Gunnars. Winnipeg: Turnstone Press, 1988, 133-46.

Vauthier, Simone. "Images in Stones, Images in Words: Margaret Laurence's *The Stone Angel*." In *Critical Approaches to the Writing of Margaret Laurence*. Ed. Colin Nicholson. Vancouver: University of British Columbia Press, 1990, 46-70.

Wainwright, J.A. "'You Have to Go Home Again': Art and Life in *The Diviners*." *World Literature Written in English* 20, 2 (1981): 292-311.

Warwick, Susan. *The River of Now and Then: The Diviners*. Toronto: ECW Press, 1993.

Williams, David. *Confessional Fictions: A Portrait of the Artist in the Canadian Novel*. Toronto: University of Toronto Press, 1991.

BIBLIOGRAPHY

Woodcock, George, ed. *A Place to Stand On: Essays by and about Margaret Laurence*. Edmonton: NeWest Press, 1983.

Woodward, Kathleen. "Late Theory, Late Style: Loss and Renewal in Freud and Barthes." In *Aging and Gender in Literature: Studies in Creativity*. Ed. Anne M. Brown and Janice Rossen. Charlottesville and London: University Press of Virgina, 1993, 82-101.

INDEX

A

Absence, 122
Act of writing, 92
Abdication of authority, 73
Address to the dead, 37
"Adonais," 76, 143, 160, 164
Adultery, 70, 82, 84
Aeschylus, 4
Afterlife, 104, 105, 143
Agamemnon, 79
Aging, 16, 24, 29, 30, 34
Ambiguous endings, Laurence's
    novels, 146-148
Anderson, Jessica, 4
Ariès, Philip, 47, 48, 53, 158,
    159
Aristotle, 168
Arnold, Matthew, 76, 143, 164
Articulation
    and desire, 51, 56
    of self-awareness, 51
    of sexual desire, 54
Attig, Thomas, 15, 151, 155
Auden, W.H., 4
Autobiography, 4-6
Aversion to physical weakness,
    26
Awakening self, 46

B

Babette's Feast, 112
Badlands, 151
Bailey, Nancy, 159
Bakhtin, Mikhail, 50-52, 159
Beattie, Ann, 4
Beckman-Long, Brenda, 155
Bell, Alice, 25, 156
Beowulf, 151
Bereavement, 6, 37
Bevan, Allan, 162
Bildungsroman, 110, 141

Bion, 142
Body
    decline of, 22-23, 28, 29
    failure of, 21, 30, 140
Bowering, George, 159
Bowlby, John, 8, 12, 14-15, 54,
    152, 154-155, 159
Burial, 59-60, 131, 132
Buss, Helen, 46, 118, 157, 159,
    167

C

Catharsis, 9, 35
Cave, Terence, 169
Cemeteries, see graveyards
Challenges to conventional
    mourning, 108
Chew, Shirley, 155
Children and funerals, 106
Clayton, John J., 11, 154
Codification of death, 60
Confessional memoir, 94
Conflicted feelings about
    parents, 55
Confrontations with loss, 9
Conscious mourning, 7
Consolation, 8, 12, 37, 70, 71,
    80, 86, 90, 93, 102, 114,
    115, 118, 122, 130, 133,
    135, 140
Cook, Méira, 116, 165, 167
Corpses, 29, 122-124, 127
Creativity, 11, 112, 116-117, 137
Crenshaw, David A., 152

D

Dante, 4
"Darkling Thrush, The," 145
Darling, Michael, 101, 163, 164
Davidson, Arnold E., 92, 163
Death, 3, 4, 26, 48, 86, 97
    acceptance of, 21, 39-40
    and animals, 130

INDEX

WRITING GRIEF

WRITING GRIEF

*Margaret Laurence
and the Work of Mourning*

Christian Riegel

UNIVERSITY OF MANITOBA PRESS

© Christian Riegel 2003

University of Manitoba Press
Winnipeg, Manitoba R3T 2N2 Canada
www.umanitoba.ca/uofmpress
Printed in Canada on acid-free paper by Friesens.

Cover Design: Doowah Design
Text Design: Sharon Caseburg
Cover Photo: Greg Klassen

National Library of Canada Cataloguing in Publication Data

Riegel, Christian Erich, 1968-
  Writing grief : Margaret Laurence and the work of mourning / Christian Riegel.

  Includes bibliographical references and index.
  ISBN 0-88755-673-6

  1. Laurence, Margaret, 1926-1987--Criticism and interpretation. 2. Grief in literature. I. Title.
  PS8523.A86Z825 2003   C813'.54   C2003-911068-0

The University of Manitoba Press gratefully acknowledges the financial support for its publication program provided by the Government of Canada through the Book Publishing Industry Development Program (BPIDP); the Canada Council for the Arts; the Manitoba Arts Council; and the Manitoba Department of Culture, Heritage and Tourism.

This book has been published with the help of a grant from the Canadian Federation for the Humanities and Social Sciences, through the Aid to Scholarly Publications Programme, using funds provided by the Social Sciences and Humanities Research Council of Canada.